POWER to CHANGE

Breaking the Destructive Patterns in Your Life!

Jason Frenn

Foreword by Paul Finkenbinder

Summit Books, LLC

Power to change
Jason Frenn

Copyright © 2005 Jason Frenn

Summit Books
60 E. Simpson Ave
PO Box 2869
Jackson WY 83001

Editor: Stephen Larson
Cover design: Brian Kramer
Interior design: arte@peniel.com

ISBN 987-2239-90-8

2nd Edition 2005

Printed in Colombia

Dedicated to:

A great person

A great Christian

A great example

A great mom

ROBERTA HART

Acknowledgements

Thank you Cindee for all of your dedication to helping me be the best person I can be. You have been my best friend and spouse for seventeen years. Aside from eternal life, you are the greatest gift that God could have given me. Thank you for everything.

Thank you Celina, Chanel and Jazmin for having the patience with daddy during the months it took to put this book together. Thank you for pulling me away from my laptop and making me play baseball with you in the street. All three of you are some of the greatest people I have ever known, and I love you with all my heart.

Thank you mom for the many years of laughter and love. You did a great job raising me and providing an environment where I could develop the talents that God gave me. You have made me a very proud son. Also, thank you for giving me accurate information regarding this book. Without you or your wonderful testimony, it would never have become a reality. Nor would it have helped the tens of thousands of people who need help.

Thank you dad, for all the after school playground experiences and making me proud to see my dad hit it over the play ground fence. Thank you for being a great dad and making an extra-ordinary effort to be there during times of family turbulence and struggle. Thank you for all thousands of hours of travel you have invested to see me (when I was a child) and my family (as I began in ministry, traveling to Central America). You are definitely part of what Tom Brokaw calls "The Greatest Generation!"

Thank you Brian and Haidee for a great design on the cover. Thank you for standing between the living and the dead with Cindee and me proclaiming the Gospel of Hope to people who desperately need to hear that Christ has come to set the captive free.

Thank you Stephen Larson for being a wonderful brother-in-law and for editing this text. I appreciate all the long hard hours you invested to make this a better document. I can tell that God has gifted you in many areas.

Thank you Doug Brendel and Tracy Borchart and our friends at Berkey, Brendel and Sheline for your outstanding assistance in the layout and flow of this book. There are few words that describe my gratitude. I know that many more lives will be touched as a direct result of your work.

A special thank you to the Assemblies of God World Missions leadership (CRFF, Paul & Karla Weis, Dick Nicholson & EXCOMM and everyone in between). People have said over the years that we have one of the most special missionary organization/families around. I must agree. Thank you for standing by Cindee and me and for supporting a ministry that no one ever thought would get off the ground.

Gracias a mis queridos suegros: Richard and Janice Larson for raising the perfect helpmate for me. You are wonderful people, filled with integrity, character and love for those who need the Lord. I cease to be amazed by the quality of people you are. I am highly privileged to have you as family.

Thank you to our advisory board: Don Judkins, Wayne Kraiss, Bruce Van Hal, Paul Weis, Fred Cottriel, Dick Larson and every member who has come along side of the vision God has placed in our hearts.

Finally, to the Taking it to the Nations staff and volunteers in Costa Rica and in Orange County, CA. We love you all and are so proud to be a part of the ministry that the Lord is developing in you. Without you, the past five years of exciting ministry would never have been the same. You are more than co-laborers. You are family and friends.

JASON FRENN

Contents

FOREWORD

Dr. Paul Finkenbinder

"Do you want to experience a new life?" The question came out of the dark in the midst of a winter gathering in the San Bernardino Mountains of Southern California. The young lad who heard the voice was only fifteen years of age. A friend had invited him to a church meeting, and church was not part of his normal life. Church, in fact, was hardly encouraged, and had never been a part of his family life.

Besides the fear of stepping into what for him was a strange environment, the lights in the building suddenly went dark. In fact the "blackout" affected a large area of the town. Electricity did return, but it was in the midst of this confusion that he hears the question: "Do you want to experience a new life?"

Never has humanity been more in need of "a new life" then today. My wife and I were flying from John Wayne airport in Orange County, California to Santa Cruz, Bolivia. After obtaining our boarding passes we were directed to go to the line that led to the "security checkpoint". John Wayne airport is not a large international airport, but there were already many hundreds waiting in line. It took us over one hour of slow plodding to finally get to the checkpoint where our hand luggage and our persons were meticulously scrutinized. I've been traveling by every means known, especially by air, for over 60 years and have never experienced such incredibly thorough inspection. What is taking place? What's happened to our freedoms? Where is the peaceful living that we knew just a few years ago? And where is all this taking us to?

Besides the general confusion that has become a part of life, something worse is happening. It's the confusion that rests within the heart and mind of the individual. People today, as never before, are subjected to such pressures, that not only is nervous breakdown a common occurrence but sadly, many feel that the only solution to life's wrenching struggles is suicide.

How do we climb out of this miry clay that has us sinking deeper and deeper into endless despair?

A nephew of mine and his wife visited us a few days ago. We hadn't seen them for several years. They had with them a four-year-old child, a little girl with beautiful eyes, blond hair and a smile that would wrench any adult's heart. No sooner had they entered the door of our home the little child came over to where I stood and just hung on to my leg. I didn't know her story yet, but I couldn't help but wonder why she stayed so close.

The child was not theirs. They had only had her a few months. The little girl, though she was only four years old, had been in four foster homes before being taken in by my nephew and his wife, her present guardians. I asked about the background of the child. Her biological mother, who had her out of wedlock, was addicted to alcohol and drugs, and her wayward lifestyle was more important to her than was caring for this beautiful little girl. The child had been abandoned several times, and after living in several foster homes "Social Services" called my nephew and his wife. Now, this one child at least, has a promising future.

The young man who heard the call: "Do you want to experience a new life?" was Jason Frenn, the author of the book you hold in your hands. His background and his young-life experiences, many of which were damaging if not totally destructive, gave him powerful insights into the problems that plague today's society. Feeling a strong necessity to share the truths he has found, he projects to you the question that as a 15 year-old lad he heard: "Do you want to experience a new life?"

Read these pages with somber reflection and you too will find that "promising future" that can be yours.

Introduction

It's all too wonderful for me!

I once had a social science professor who would say, "It's all too wonderful for me."

That was his response whenever he found himself in a verbal dispute without an answer to a complex question.

As we look for answers in this complex world, we too might say, "It's all too wonderful for me."

The world we live in is complicated, and many struggle to understand it.

Wars start as planes are flown into office buildings.

Hate permeates the planet like a virus seeking to devour everything in its path.

Thousands take their lives each year, seeking relief from their tremendous emotional pain.

As we turn on the news we see one tragedy after another, in a society yearning to find meaning and answers.

In the major metropolitan areas of the world, gangs are growing at an astronomical pace.

The violent crime rate is climbing.

The divorce rate leans over the fifty percent mark in many countries, and domestic violence is on the rise.

Families across the U.S. continue to disintegrate despite the good intentions of a conservative movement seeking to bring change through legislation and political action.

Kids are being introduced to drugs, sex and violence earlier in life.

Parents find it difficult to talk to their children, and children find it hard to be understood and accepted by their parents.

Most kids would agree that watching their favorite television program is better without their parents around.

Generation gaps that used to split every thirty to forty years now split every three to four years.

Is it all too wonderful for you?

Do the problems of life overwhelm you?

Are you looking for answers to your complex life?

Have you ever said to yourself, "Stop the world, I need to step off!"

Are you standing on sinking sand?

Are you having difficulty holding on to something concrete?

Does anxiety govern your decisions and fears determine your plans?

Are you caught in the same vicious cycle and patterns you've been stuck in for years?

Do you ask yourself, "Will it ever end?"

Are there issues in your life you've never been able to resolve?

Take a good hard look at the person in the mirror.

Ask yourself if you are truly living or simply surviving?

Are you living the life you've always wanted to live?

Are you free or are you bound?

Do you enjoy life or are you dominated by it?

Do you determine your destiny or do others?

Are you in control or is your life manipulated by circumstances, other people, or personal patterns of destruction.

Only one person can answer these questions: you.

You alone have the answers to these questions.

You are not alone

These questions may be difficult to answer, but you are not alone.

If the soul searching provoked by these questions has left you with the overwhelming sense that you don't have it all together, don't worry.

There are over six billion other people on the planet, and they are in the same boat.

The most crucial question is: "What are you going to do about it?"

Will you consider change or continue in the same helpless, victimized state?

If you desire to change, I have good news for you.

God grants the *power to change* to those who ask Him.

God desires you to live life, not just survive it.

He desires you to live a life of freedom, not oppression — strength and courage, not fear and anxiety — joy and satisfaction, not depression and discontent.

This book focuses first and foremost on personal change.

It deals with God's redemptive power to help us break the chains of destructive patterns handed down from generation to generation.

The same ruinous habits that we see in our parents and grandparents find roadways into our being and settle into our daily life.

Like cancers, they spread from one generation to the next, keeping their victims in vicious cycles of helplessness.

Many times, we can be blind not only to their presence

but also to their enormous power over us.

Although we promise ourselves that we will never become like our parents, with time, we discover that the same tendencies begin to surface in our own lives.

Many of us adopt habits from our parents that keep us locked into cycles of destruction.

For instance, sociologists will tell you that sixty percent of those born into homes with an addiction will find that the cycle repeats itself.

Sixty percent of those born into alcoholic homes have a tendency to become alcoholics.

Sixty percent of those born into homes of drug abuse struggle with the same vice in their own lives.

Sixty percent of those born into homes with eating disorders struggle with food.

The same could be said about divorce, physical abuse, neglect and depression.

Importantly, this book is not a "parental blaming" session.

Most parents are wonderful gifts from God, who want the best for their children.

However, like every previous generation, they are part of a long history of dysfunction embedding itself through culture.

Most parents do the best with what they have.

They are not to be accused or rebuked.

Parents are to be honored, by taking the good handed down to us, cutting away destructive patterns, and setting healthy ones into motion.

By doing this, God will produce in us a generation, followed by others, that can love and appreciate its past instead of being bitter or resentful.

The point is that we should build on the good nature of our parents and believe that God will break the domino effect that has handicapped past generations.

In the cases where few, if any, destructive patterns are present, He can help prevent the problems from starting in us (the first generation).

These are not issues found exclusively in homes where there is no religious affiliation.

These are problems found both inside and outside of the church.

Ordinary people who attend church as well as those who do not, constantly face issues such as those mentioned above.

For this reason, this book is written for all of humanity and is not aimed at one particular sector of the population.

God loves everyone, and it is for everyone that this book has been written.

Most importantly, this book was written for you!

You have a partner

The heart of this book is to challenge you to change yourself.

Take the reins of your own life.

Stop blaming others or looking for excuses.

Take responsibility for your own actions, lifestyle, reactions and habits.

In order for this to happen, it is imperative that you form an alliance with God.

You and God are the two most important ingredients in changing your life.

He has sovereign power to dynamically transform you.

At the same time, He has granted you the freedom to choose whether or not to change.

Perhaps it may seem like a dichotomy.

Try to look at it as a partnership.

If you exercise the freedom to choose God's help, He will transform and guide you through the process.

You take responsibility of your life, while granting God mastership as well.

Together, you and God are partners in accomplishing the task.

As you take responsibility for your own life and bring it to God, He will be faithful in helping you to rebuild it.

The end result is that you will live life, not simply survive it.

This partnership between you and God is absolutely essential for realizing change.

Think of it like a football team.

He is the captain, and you are the quarterback.

He gives you direction, guidance, insight and strength.

You are responsible for your position.

You do not try to play God, and He doesn't play the game for you.

Because He is a Sovereign God, He calls the plays.

That's why He's the coach.

You can refuse what He suggests, because you, the player, have a free will.

However, He will not implement the play to win the game, if you refuse to cooperate, and ultimately the entire team will lose.

However, if you accept His guidance, insight and transformation, you will experience victory.

The key here is to form an alliance with God and be in total obedience to His word.

Doing so guarantees victory.

In the real world, God is responsible for all that is supernatural, and He doesn't want you to play God.

He just wants you to take responsibility for your own life, and be responsible for the natural realm.

I will explain five steps you can take to obtain victory over the destructive patterns handed down from generation to generation.

The first step is a radical change in perception, realizing that change is not only necessary but also possible.

Most of us recognize that change is important but find it hard to believe it is possible.

That is where the battle lies.

The second step is to work with God to manage your life by rewriting the habits and behavioral patterns of destruction handed down from past generations.

As you do this, the Lord will help you realize the root of the problem.

As you ask the Lord for help, guidance and assistance on a daily basis, you will begin to notice that the struggles you once found unbearable will become manageable.

The third step is to implement new habits into your life so that you do not fall back into the old patterns of destruction.

The fourth step is to forgive and be forgiven.

This will help you release resentment and bitterness towards others and receive freedom from past hurts.

Finally, the fifth step is to establish a network of trusted friends, so that accountability can reinforce the work that God has done in your life.

As you embark upon the path of change, God will help you overcome insurmountable odds.

The problems you face do not matter in light of who God is and His power to help you.

However the decision to do something about your life is entirely yours.

Left alone, dysfunctions have the potential of turning into monstrous or even catastrophic problems.

They can manifest themselves in addictive, abusive and destructive behaviors and eventually be passed onto the next generation, where the cycle repeats itself, at times with even greater severity.

If you want the very best for your life, read on.

I am sure that you want good and wonderful things for your family, marriage and children.

Most of us want the very best.

That desire is a godly one.

If that is your desire, do not stop halfway through this book.

Read the whole book and keep it as a reference.

You will find that as you apply the godly principles threaded throughout this book, your life will take on a whole new dimension of spiritual and psychological health.

The end result will be a whole life, a life much closer to contentment than you ever dreamed, a life of peace and significance.

I come from a home where addiction was a problem for many generations.

I can see those problems developing in my family tree since before the 1900s.

Alcoholism — depression — bitterness and hurt — confusion, anger and loneliness — all were problems.

All of these tendencies were destined to repeat themselves in my life and in my children's lives.

But that has not occurred.

What happened?

God helped me through the process of being set free.

He broke the chains of bondage and set me free from destructive behavioral patterns.

As a result, I am a healthy person.

My marriage and family are healthy.

My wife Cindee and I have three wonderful girls, all serving the Lord in ministry with us.

My relationship with my father and mother is a healthy

one.

My in-laws and I have a great relationship.

How did I get from point A to point B?

The answer lies within the pages of this book.

You too can experience God's love and life changing power that sets the captive free.

If your world is too overwhelming, if you feel stuck in patterns of destruction, if it is all too wonderful for you, there is one hope that I want to share with you.

There is hope in Jesus.

There is hope for anyone, regardless of their background or circumstances.

The choice is yours.

This is my prayer for you: I pray that Jesus would set you free from the cycles of destructive patterns handed down from generation to generation and from the struggles in which you find yourself.

As we embark upon this journey together, these are Jesus' words to you: "The Spirit of the Lord is on me, because He has anointed me to preach good news to the poor.

He has sent me to proclaim freedom for the prisoners and recovery of sight to the blind, to release the oppressed, to proclaim the acceptable year of the Lord's favor." Luke 4:18,19.

Chapter 1

Pull over and ask for directions

Pulling over and asking for directions does not come easy for most.

We like to think that we've got it all under control.

You might think, "Why ask for directions? If I keep driving, I'll get there soon enough. I'll just drive a little faster, and that should solve the problem."

In fact, asking someone for directions implies you don't know how to get to your destination.

You might feel embarrassed or inadequate.

After all, we don't want people to think that we can't make it on our own.

You don't want anyone to think you're lost.

Try to look at it from another angle.

Asking for directions is not a sign of weakness.

It's a sign of healthiness.

Recognizing the fact that we might be lost, and then turning to someone for help is the first step towards recovery.

Gaining better insight is healthy.

The fact that you are reading this book is a healthy sign.

Considering the dips and windy turns we face, asking for directions could save your career, marriage, family and life.

Imagine a 747 taking off from Los Angeles and heading to New York.

Several minutes into the flight, the pilot discovers that the onboard navigational system has failed, and he loses all instrumentation.

Because he is embarrassed to ask for help, he decides to fly the plane without any assistance.

He asks the other pilots to leave the cockpit and locks the door.

After all, he's flown that route before.

He then does the unthinkable and refuses to radio air traffic control and tell them the problem.

He has no idea how high or how fast he is flying.

He has very little idea in which direction he is flying.

Nonetheless, he believes he can fly in the dark over 2,500 miles and safely land in rainy weather on the other side of the country.

Sound ridiculous?

I am sure you would never want to be on that flight.

Who would?

Still, that is how millions of people manage their lives on a daily basis.

Just like the pilot, they are afraid to ask for help.

For some, they are unaware that they have lost their way.

They have no idea what's going on in their life.

Their navigational system has lost power.

They have no idea where they're going or how they're doing.

They are not managing; they're surviving.

In short, life is living them.

Without getting a better idea of who we are, it's no wonder that the complexities of life seem to be trapping so many of us.

Being in tune with your navigational system is imperative.

Simply put, it's being in tune with yourself.

It guides you through the turbulence of life.

You may not be able to control the weather, but you know exactly where you are flying and how to get to your destination.

As you face trials and difficulties with personal relationships, your navigational system helps you work out the flight pattern of life.

Perhaps the people you work with are hostile or rude.

You may be living in the clutches of poverty or in a highly dysfunctional home.

You could be surviving a destructive relationship.

Perhaps your children are rebellious, or your marriage is a disaster.

You might have no education.

Your relationship with your parents might be severed.

Maybe you were abused or struggle with an identity crisis.

Perhaps you have a terrible debilitating addiction.

Your self-esteem might be low, or perhaps you're living in depression.

The issue at hand isn't how these issues are affecting you, but rather how you manage them.

If you are unable to manage, you are not living life but surviving it.

All of these outside forces are manageable, provided you take control over how you react to them.

You may not be able to control the circumstances that surround you at any given moment.

You can decide, however, how you will react to them.

Remember the pilot?

He could have chosen to radio for help.

He could have kept his crew in the cockpit.

But because of his fear of humiliation, he chose to react in a negative way.

In doing so, he not only put his own life at risk but the life of every passenger onboard.

We have the power to choose how to react: as a victim or as a victor.

The choice is yours.

If you choose not to change, circumstances and people will continue to carve out a destiny of struggle and misery for you.

When you do not determine your destiny, other people and circumstances will.

A while back I saw a news report on a girl who was afraid to leave her house in South Central Los Angeles.

She had allegedly been locked in by her mother and not allowed to leave for an extended period of time.

The house was rat infested and should have been condemned.

According to the reporter, the girl was afraid of leaving the house because she had hardly been allowed outside.

The loud noises and the brightness outside scared her, and thus reinforced her paranoia.

Occasionally, she peaked through a small window to view with caution what was occurring out in the street or in front of her house.

An anonymous neighbor saw her several times and reported it to the authorities.

The family had been investigated several years before, but the authorities had not considered the living circumstances to be detrimental to the girl or the family.

This time, however, the social worker took the girl and placed her with social services.

Fear is the number one paralyzer that keeps people

locked in to where they are.

Because of fear, people cannot improve, recover or heal.

P E R C E P T I O N S

You can only see what you are willing to see

We live in a life full of difficulties, challenges and opportunities.

I have learned through my travels, speaking engagements and studies that most problems are not on the outside.

They are on the inside.

The problem does not entangle us.

Trials or difficulties do not hold us hostage.

We are not bound from the outside.

We are bound on the inside.

How?

Our emotional vision gets clouded with destructive thought patterns that keep us in the same cycles for years.

We interpret problems as an external force beyond our control, when, in fact, the way we approach the problem *is* the problem.

That is not to say that external problems or difficulties do not set us back.

Everyone goes through tough times.

However, one underlying fact remains.

Your reactions to problems are heavily determined by your navigational system.

What is your navigational system?

In short, it is your perception.

It guides you.

It directs you.

Your perception is the biggest factor in how you will react to problems.

Note that perception is not to be confused with perspective.

There is an important distinction between perspective and perception.

Perspective is a point from which we view something, figuratively or literally.

It's the angle from which we see a house, building, sky, physical objects or personalities, problems, situations.

However perception is how our mind interprets the data entering our mind from any given perspective.

Perception embraces all that your senses feed into your mind and helps the mind interpret that data.

Imagine that you have the best seat in the stadium to watch the Super bowl (a great perspective on the game).

You are situated about twenty rows back so that you have a good perspective in relationship to height and depth to the field.

You are seated in the shade so the sun is not blinding.

Your seat is perfectly centered between both end zones.

Then, as the game starts, you slip on a welder's shield.

Although you barely see everything, it is so dark and distorted; you can't really understand what's happening.

You hear the roar of the crowd as one team approaches the other's goal line.

You obviously cannot enjoy the game.

What will your perception of the game be?

Dark, confusing and at times noisy!

Although you were in a wonderful position and could potentially view the game from a great perspective, your perception of the game was heavily tainted.

In the same way, our perspective in life and

personal relationships are greatly affected by our perceptions.

Many of us are educated.

Some may be wealthy.

Others may have grown up in wonderful homes.

Those things may have positioned us for a wonderful life, but unless our perceptions are correct, the way we interpret life will be contorted.

For that reason, there are those who are affluent, educated and intelligent but who find it difficult to stop the craziness in their lives.

How many times have we turned on the news only to hear that another wealthy movie star has been arrested on drug possession?

How many times have we seen a comedian or rock star overdose on narcotics?

The lenses they are wearing may have been chosen by them, or may have been handed to them by past generations, and they greatly affect the way they see life.

Although they supposedly "had it all," their perceptions guided them to destruction.

On the other hand, we see many people coming from the worst socioeconomic conditions known to man, who overcome insurmountable odds to become highly effective individuals, parents and spouses.

The difference wasn't where they were placed in life (their perspective), but how they viewed and interpreted life (their perception).

Many of us know the story of Moses.

In the land of Egypt, a decree was issued to kill every first-born Israelite.

Shortly after his birth, his mother sent him in a basket down the river Nile, in order to flee from Pharaoh's wrath.

He was miraculously found by Pharaoh's daughter, who decided to adopt him.

He was born in a poor home, but he spent his adolescent years in the palace.

The Bible says that after he saw an Egyptian punishing an Israelite, he welled up with anger and killed the Egyptian.

For fear that he would lose his life, he fled into the desert.

Once again he found himself living in poverty.

He knew no one, and started life all over again.

During Moses' exile, Rameses came into power as Pharaoh.

As far as world politics were concerned, he held the most powerful position on the planet.

Moses, on the other hand, was in a different place in life.

I am sure that he was depressed, lonely and needed desperately to have his navigational system repaired.

Little did Moses know that he was about to have his perceptions turned upside down.

One day, on a mountain, he had an encounter with God in a burning bush.

The Lord told him that He had heard the weeping of the people of Israel: "I have indeed seen the misery of my people in Egypt. I have heard them crying out because of their slave drivers. And I am concerned about their suffering. So I have come down to rescue them from the hand of the Egyptians and to bring them up out of that land into a good and spacious land, a land flowing with milk and honey."

The Lord says, "I want you to go."

Moses said to God, "Who am I, that I should go to Pharaoh and bring the Israelites out of Egypt?"

God replied, "I will be with you."

He emphasized once again that Moses was God's choice to lead the nation of Israel out of the clutches of slavery.

Moses suggested that he was not a man of eloquent speech and implied that the Israelites would not follow him.

I am sure Moses thought, "I can barely lead myself."

But God said, "I am the God of Abraham, Isaac and Jacob."

He is the almighty.

Forever the world will remember Him as the great I AM.

He is the creator of the universe.

So He reiterates, "I am sending you, Moses. Fear not, I am with you."

An army wasn't necessary — God's presence was the only essential.

Moses got the picture.

He realized that God is bigger than our circumstances.

He had a radical encounter that produced a radical transformation in his perception.

Moses returned to Egypt and led his nation out of the oppressive hands of the Egyptians.

He did so with the vengeance of 10 unparalleled plagues that left their mark in the history books.

He defeated Rameses, as God demonstrated His omnipotent power.

Unlike Rameses, Moses was arguably one of the most influential people in the history of the world.

There are maybe one or two persons that have had the impact that Moses had.

He was born into poverty and visited it on more than one occasion.

The perspective from which he was born was of poverty and slavery.

But with God, he overcame insurmountable odds.

Pharaoh, on the other hand, is only mentioned within the pages of Egyptian history and in the context of his own dynasty.

Pharaoh was born in the palace.

He was born rich.

He had everything.

He had glory and even a "godly" status.

His position was great.

His perspective was great.

But compared to Moses, he had little impact upon the world.

In the end, God defeated Rameses, and Rameses is remembered as the Pharaoh who let the Israelites get away.

What was the difference between Moses and Rameses?

Moses had an encounter with the living God at the burning bush.

The encounter was so impressive that it literally transformed Moses from head to toe.

God took a man born of poverty, a man who gained much and lost it all, and transformed him into one of the greatest leaders the world has ever seen.

Moses not only realized that he needed to change, but he recognized that change was possible.

He was flexible and obedient.

These are the two most important ingredients for realizing the power to change.

If we desire to live life and not simply survive it, we need to ask God to help us change our perceptions.

We need to remove the welder's shield from our eyes in order to appreciate a better perspective.

This helps us change the manner in which we see and react to the world around us.

We can address problems in a different light, if we see them clearly with a godly perception.

In order for us to see the problem differently, we need to be different.

Once we are different and our perceptions change, we can experience every great promise God has for us, including breaking the chains of generational sins and destructive patterns.

For this reason it is absolutely essential to see things with a godly perception.

P E R C E P T I O N S

Seeing people for who they are

Having a godly perception helps the way you perceive your family, work, children, spouse, God and friends.

I say that because your perceptions also determine how you interact in personal relationships.

Your child, for example, might have tremendous potential, but if you never look for it, chances are you will never help him or her take advantage of it.

And our failure to see such potential could initiate destructive patterns into their thought processes.

Children pick up on subtleties.

They can sense the meaning of our silence or what we think about them.

We shouldn't pretend for a moment that our loved ones cannot discern how we perceive them.

Perhaps your perception tells you that your child is hyper.

He may have attention deficit disorder.

He might be a problem child.

He can't get along with other kids.

In fact, however, he might have an enormous amount of energy waiting to be discovered.

He might be a late bloomer.

He could grow up to be the next Leonardo Da Vinci.

Many children who are categorized and brushed aside as lost causes turn out to be world changers, once their true potential is discovered.

The first step is removing the welder's shield from our own eyes so that we can see our world with God's perspective.

One of the subtle hints in Jesus' analogy of removing the speck from your brother's eye after you remove the beam from your own, suggests that you have no true perception to help others until you remove that which is hindering your vision.

Jesus says in Luke 6:42, "How can you say to your brother, 'Brother, let me take the speck out of your eye,' when you yourself fail to see the plank in your own eye? You hypocrite, first take the plank out of your eye, and then you will see clearly to remove the speck from your brother's eye."

The Bibles says in II Corinthians 4:4 that "the god of this age (Satan) has blinded the minds of unbelievers, so they cannot see the light of the gospel of the glory of Christ, who is the image of God."

Satan's task is to contort our perception.

He blinds us and paints a picture of helplessness so that eventually we lose our perspective.

God's work starts with correcting perception.

When God starts to work with an individual, He almost always begins with his or her perception.

Take this biblical fact for example: Of all the healings Jesus performed, He healed blind people more than any other type of healing recorded in the New Testament.

Of all those who God used in the Bible, Jesus was the only one who healed the blind.

This has not only physical implications but spiritual and psychological ones as well.

God is the expert in giving sight to the blind, and He also heals our perceptions.

What does this subtle biblical fact suggest?

God can change your worldview, your perception and ultimately the way you react to the world around you.

When we have a radical shift in perception, the scales fall, and we can see our life for what it is.

We can see God's plan and His blessings for us as we seek Him.

We can grasp the great potential that has lain dormant for years.

Once our vision is clear, we can move towards recovery and living life as God intended us to live.

You might be asking, "What are those issues that block our vision and affect our perception?"

They are thought and behavioral patterns engraved into our mind, soul and spirit.

It's the way we think.

And the way we think strongly determines who and what we are.

I will never forget the first time I was invited to church by my neighbors.

I was 15 years of age, a sophomore in high school.

It was a snowy night.

The temperature was about 28 degrees.

I rarely attended church.

From time to time I went to a typical Easter morning celebration.

For the most part, I spent Sundays doing whatever came my way.

My family wasn't religious in any sense of the word.

So I admit that I felt a little uncomfortable walking into that old Christian Missionary Alliance church.

I followed my friends to the second row.

"The second row! Man alive," I thought. "Couldn't we have sat a little further back? Everyone here knows that I'm new. They'll be staring at me the whole night."

Within several minutes of the opening song, a power failure affected the entire block.

I was a bit nervous.

I thought that I was such a depraved adolescent that I had obviously blown the transformer with my bad vibes.

So there I was, sitting in the second row, everyone staring at me, and realizing that I must have damaged the power grid.

To make things worse my neighbor leaned over and said, "You know, that never happened until you walked in the building."

I knew that he was joking, but my self-esteem was as low as low could be.

I felt embarrassed.

My perception was clouded with self-doubt and humiliation.

Did anyone cause this?

Of course not!

Those were my perceptions.

I carried them into the building.

No matter what anyone could have said, my perception was tainted by a heavy welder's shield.

I thought, "Well, this service is ruined."

Then something interesting happened.

The pastor signaled for someone to bring in the candles from the storage facility.

He said, "This is not the first blackout we've seen in Big Bear, and it certainly will not be the last."

The ushers placed about 20 candles throughout the sanctuary.

It provided enough light for all 150 of us to read the passages of the Bible being shared.

Although it started out as a turbulent service, the pastor guided us through a calm and insightful message.

He talked about a God who loves and doesn't condemn.

He shared with us a Christ who died for the iniquities and sins of the world.

He shared with us a God who had the power to transform any individual and give him or her eternal life.

He talked about a God who brings the meaning of life back to life.

He then asked a question, "Don't you want to experience new life?"

Hearing those words for the first time caused a radical shift in the way I think.

It was as though the light went on in my head.

I saw things through different lenses.

The welder's shield was lifted, and I could see things from God's perspective.

It's the difference between swimming in a pool without a mask and then putting one on.

Everything becomes clear.

It was an epiphany.

"Hold on a second!" I thought. "God has the power to change anyone. And that anyone can be me. God has the power to help us change our perceptions, including mine. God grants eternal life. He can grant me eternal life."

I walked out of that church a changed teenager.

God began a work in me that is strong to this very day.

He changed my perception, and in doing so He changed the way I think.

By changing the way I think, He changed who I am.

God has the ability to turn on the light.

He can assist you in changing your perceptions.

Our challenge is to remove the welder's shield.

Allow God to assist you in changing the way you think.

You cannot do it alone.

Remember, it's a partnership.

God has the power, but you have freewill.

The choice is yours.

You have no idea what a tremendous future God has in store for you.

As your perceptions change you will begin to grasp the great possibilities that God will bring to life.

The first step in the power to change is recognizing that you have a problem.

It's the problem of poor perception that doesn't allow you to fulfill your great potential that God has for you.

Something is wrong.

You might not know exactly what it is.

But something isn't right.

Admitting there's a problem is essential.

That is why understanding your own perception is so important.

You can't help someone who doesn't think there is a problem.

Just like the pilot, helping someone on a course of self-destruction is impossible when you can't see the need for help.

Likewise, you can't help yourself, if you first can't admit that there is a problem.

Remove the welder's shield, and look at yourself for who you really are.

Be truthful.

Be honest.

You only have your life once.

Now's the time to make it right.

Make it right not only for yourself but also for your children, your children's children and for every generation that follows.

If you are like the millions upon millions each year that try to lose weight, you recognize that something isn't right.

You feel fat.

You feel uncomfortable with yourself.

You want to change.

You recognize that you need to change.

In the same way, you want change for the rest of your life.

You've come to the conclusion that change is necessary.

You're just not sure how, or if it's possible.

The purpose of this book is to communicate this simple fact to you: Jesus has come to set the captive free.

Your circumstances do not matter.

Your past makes no difference in light of who God is.

If you are captive and desire change, place your trust in the Savior.

There is hope in Jesus.

You might ask, "How?"

It begins with an encounter.

Much like the encounter that Moses had with the burning bush, you come as you are.

God does not require that you change yourself before meeting Him.

Meeting Him changes who you are.

You begin with a conversation with God.

You might start off by saying:

> "Lord, I am not quite sure how I arrived or exactly where I am going, but one thing is for certain.

I need your help to get there.

I need you to change my heart.

I need you to change my mind.

I need you to change my perception.

Help me to see things with your perception.

I want a godly perception.

I recognize that I cannot do it alone.

I need your help.

I am sorry for all the damage I have done to those around me.

I commit myself to a relationship with you and embark upon an adventure of getting to know you.

Most importantly, I commit myself to whatever you ask of me during this process of change.

Help me to be strong, obedient, and open to your change for my life.

Make yourself real to me with each passing day.

I pray these things in Christ's name.

Amen."

Chapter 2

When I grow up, I'm going to be different than my parents...

Tears slid down her cheek as she sat in the dark cold closet.

Once again, loneliness and confusion embraced her heart as she experienced the abuse of being locked in a closet by her older siblings.

Periodically, she could hear them working on their chores.

She continued to whimper.

Finally, an older sibling sternly spoke to her through the door: "We'll let you out, but only if you stop crying. If we hear more than a peep out of you, you'll be in there all night! Get the picture?"

This happened from time to time in Gene's childhood.

She was the youngest of 12 siblings, and half of her brothers and sisters died from illnesses at the turn of the century.

Her mother was incapable of taking care of her, because of her old age, and had many problems of her own.

Furthermore, Gene's father passed away when she was

a little girl.

The family was being torn apart by the absence of healthy paternal figures.

She experienced many conflicts, arguments and disputes during the sixteen years she lived at home.

In Gene's case, more was happening to her than simply abuse and occasional closet detention.

She learned to protect herself from those who hurt her by forming an emotional wall to numb the pain she was experiencing.

Many times she felt herself saying, "I will never treat my husband and children like this!"

She married very early in life, but her marriage ended abruptly in divorce.

Almost a decade later, she married for the second time.

She had two children from her previous marriage and two with her second husband.

Let me underscore that she was a good person who wanted to raise her family differently from the way she was raised.

Unfortunately, she began to repeat some of the same cycles she endured during her childhood.

Her first divorce uncovered the deep wounds in her self-esteem from her childhood, which fueled a perpetuating negative self-talk.

Her second marriage would be no different.

Her husband worked at TRW, a company that installed radar systems in most of the major airports around the United States in the 1950s.

He worked over sixty hours a week at the office and more in his office at home.

As Gene's two older children eventually moved out on their own, she began to experience deeper loneliness and alienation.

This caused her to cling to her youngest daughter.

Up until Roberta was thirteen, she had a good

relationship with her mother.

In 1960, the family received a devastating phone call.

Isabel, Roberta's older sibling, was killed in an automobile accident.

As you can imagine, this sent shockwaves through the entire family, and within the few minutes of a single phone call, everyone's lives were changed forever.

"How could this happen? How could God let this happen? Why did this happen?"

These were the questions that haunted the family for years.

And as a result of this tragedy, Gene's loneliness continued to grow.

As Roberta entered high school, however, she desired to spend more time with her friends and less time at home.

Thus, Gene became controlling and, at times, physically aggressive.

Sometimes, Roberta came home from school, and her mother would be upset.

Gene would accuse her of doing things that she had not done.

In a rage, Gene would grab the nearest object and hurl it at her in an explosion of anger.

Because of the turmoil, Roberta began to pull away from her family looking for ways to escape.

She would spend more and more time away from home.

At the same time, her parents fell into continual patterns of dispute and quarrel.

Through all the emotional and physical abuse, Roberta learned to protect herself from those who hurt her by forming an emotional wall to numb the pain she experienced.

Many times she felt herself saying, "I will never treat my husband and children like this."

At age seventeen, on the night of her high school graduation, she moved out on her own to escape the dysfunction of her home.

After a short time of working and living in downtown Hollywood, she discovered what many college students discover about living in a costly culture for more than a week: It's expensive!

Thus, she had to move back home and take another job, working as a hostess in a restaurant in the San Fernando Valley.

It was there that she met her husband, who was a bartender.

Bob was a funny guy who enjoyed telling jokes and making his customers laugh.

Roberta and Bob were married and later had a baby boy.

I was that baby boy.

Three years after their marriage ceremony, and deciding that things were not working out, they were separated.

My father moved in with my grandmother, while my mother and I lived in the west end of the San Fernando Valley.

My dad was a very good father and made an attempt to see me every day after school before he went to work every night at the bar.

He loved me and expressed it from time to time.

My mom was a great parent as well.

Up until I was twelve, she spent countless hours on the road taking me to baseball practice and hockey games.

She encouraged me to play the drums and arranged for me to take horseback riding lessons.

She granted me many freedoms and encouraged my development in several areas of life.

Together, we had fun.

I can remember many summer nights barbecuing under the star filled skies of Southern California and staying up late with her watching the Saturday night lineup on television.

Those were some of the best memories of my life.

All and all, she was a great mom and did a great job raising me as a single parent.

I grew up respecting authority and others.

In 1978, I turned twelve.

In December of that year we moved to Big Bear, California.

That was a major turning point in my relationship with both my father and mother.

Because of the distance between the San Fernando Valley and Big Bear, my father saw me only two times per month (every other Sunday afternoon).

I had to face an important loss ... the loss of my father.

Before, I had seen my father once a day for several hours.

All of a sudden, I could see him for only five hours every two weeks.

Every time he left to return home, I sat in the driveway with tears in my eyes, wondering why life had stabbed me with a dagger in the heart.

My mother had problems of her own.

Living in a mountain resort community was not only boring, but very lonely.

In addition, she had difficulty making friends in the new community, and thus began to drink with frequency.

After two years, she decided to marry an old boyfriend from several years back.

The two of them matched together was like trying to put out a fire with gasoline.

In the mornings, he would complain about her drinking habit, yet would be the first one to pour her a drink in the afternoon.

In addition to the madness in their marriage, they only spent time together on the weekends.

He lived and worked in Burbank, where his business transferred film to video for the networks and occasionally the NC-17 market.

He was 32 years older than she was.

Their marriage somehow survived many roller coaster dips with many near derailments.

In the meantime, I sat on the sideline and watched my mother slip further into depression, while expressing great anger and aggression toward him.

At times, I didn't know how she survived.

Shortly after I turned fifteen, a Hispanic family living across the street from me shared the gentlest message I had ever heard.

It was the first time that I had ever heard that Jesus loved me for who I was and would never let me down.

I went to church with them and gave my heart to Christ several weeks later.

However, my parents thought that I was going through a fad.

I had many verbal disputes with my mom.

After a few drinks, she would tell me how useless my dedication to "religion" was and how ridiculous my commitment to church was.

One night, we had a heated discussion, and my patience was wearing very thin.

Finally, she said, "If you don't like it, get out!"

So I left.

I grabbed a change of clothes and got into my car and started to pull out of the garage.

As I was backing the car out, she walked out into the driveway and continued to yell at me.

Many of the neighbors came out to see all the commotion.

It was a shameful and embarrassing experience, to say the least.

One thing was amazing to me in spite of it all.

The following day when I returned, she had no recollection of what had happened the night before.

During that period in my life, I prayed for her salvation and asked God to intervene in her life.

I prayed that Jesus would walk into her life and rescue her from the destructive behavior that kept her trapped.

Yet through all the turbulence and turmoil I experienced, I never wondered why she was treating me this way.

I thought that our family was normal.

So then, in the midst of all the turbulence, I learned to protect myself from those who hurt me by forming an emotional wall to numb the pain I experienced.

Many times I felt myself saying, "I will never treat my wife and kids like this! When I grow up, I'm going to be different than my parents."

This story is the story of millions upon millions of households around the world.

My parents are great people.

I love them and deeply respect them.

They, like myself, were simply caught in cycles that started generations before they were born.

They did the best with what they had.

And from me, they get an A+.

Still, two questions remain:

How do we stop the madness?

And how do we get beyond the destruction?

The answer, in a nutshell, is that God has the power to redeem us from the patterns of bondage that have kept us from experiencing His freedom for our lives.

This is my journey.

This is my testimony.

The following pages outline the process of what God has done in me.

It points to what God can do in you to change the craziness in your generation (past, present and future) and transform your life into a blessed, meaningful and prosperous one.

That is exactly what God wants for your life.

Chapter 3

Like father like son

Most have muttered under their breath one time or another, "When I grow up, I will be different from my parents. I'm going to do things differently!"

We usually say these things under our breath when we are mad or disgusted with our parents over some embarrassing episode.

The way we talk, the way we walk, the way we react, the way we think, the way we run our lives, even the way we were raised are things we want to change as we become adults.

We make all kinds of self-promises only to discover that when we grow up, we have many of the same tendencies we despised during our younger years.

We see our parents in ourselves, and that doesn't settle well with most.

And when others say, "You're just like your father!" there is an uneasy feeling that fills our hearts.

For most adolescents, parents aren't "cool."

The thought of growing up to be just like them is frightening.

So then, if we try so hard to be different, why do so many us follow in their footsteps?

How do these patterns get handed down from one generation to the next?

Why is it so difficult to overcome that which seems to plague the family tree?

Although we try to change, although we try to shake ourselves free, although we try to break the chains, we find ourselves becoming like our parents in many ways.

Why?

The answer can be found in the book of Exodus.

There are universal spiritual laws that should not be broken.

When they are violated, it affects not only the individual but the entire family and, in many cases, generations to come.

There are processes and consequences that are irreversible, unavoidable, and unchangeable.

No matter who you are, being a human being subjects you to a process set in motion by God — a process that started when the Lord handed the Ten Commandments to Moses.

Most of the world believes in the Ten Commandments and refers to them as a basis for moral living and ethical conduct.

A vast majority of all judicial systems embrace at least half of the commandments as their starting point for the rule of law.

The two most important commandments of the ten, however, are probably the most overlooked.

They are the first and second.

I suggest that they are the most important because God, not man, placed them in that order.

As Exodus Chapter 20 begins, God establishes His right and authority to give the commandments:

Exodus 20:1, 2

Verse 1

And God spoke all these words:

Verse 2

"I am the Lord your God, who brought you out of Egypt, out of the land of slavery."

This statement demonstrates God's authority in making the following commandments.

In essence, he is saying, "I demonstrated my power over Pharaoh. I pulled you out of slavery. I sent the plagues upon Egypt. I performed miracles, signs and wonders. I delivered you from the most powerful, tyrant in the world. Therefore, I have the authority to run the show. I call the shots. Now then, this is what I want from you":

Exodus 20:3-5

Verse 3, Commandment #1

You shall have no other gods before me.

Verse 4, Commandment #2

You shall not make for yourself an idol in the form of anything in heaven above or on the earth beneath or in the waters below.

To the Lord, idol worship is a very serious offense, especially when it replaces Him as the Lord God Almighty in the life of an individual.

To this very serious transgression comes a very serious consequence.

For that reason two commandments out of the ten are dedicated to idolatry, and six verses deal with those first two commandments.

Further, God dedicates an entire verse to the repercussions of breaking the commandments.

Notice what it says in verse five:

Verse 5 Commandment #2 Cont.

You shall not bow down to them or worship them; for I, the Lord your God, am a jealous God, punishing the children for the sin of the fathers to the third and fourth generation of those who hate me.

I used to struggle with the concept of God punishing children for the sins of their parents.

How could God, a just God, punish innocent children for the mistakes of past generations?

In my pursuit of trying to understand this passage of scripture, I discovered that God isn't the one who punishes children.

He doesn't teach them how to break His laws.

He doesn't teach people how to engage in idol worship.

Parents and society do.

Parents punish their own children.

"How?" you ask.

Children grow up learning and observing the behavior of their parents.

Children absorb the habits of their caregivers as they watch them throughout life.

Someone once said that children are like video cameras with legs.

They walk around recording everything we say and do.

Parents teach us how to walk, talk, eat, relate and negotiate our way through life.

They teach us how to think about the world around us and about ourselves.

They are our models.

They can also teach us how to cheat, lie, fornicate, abuse, steal, think less of marriage, mistreat others, be hypocritical, hate ourselves or disregard the law.

Parents don't have to speak on these topics.

They don't have to vocalize what they think.

Their silent testimony, the manner in which they conduct their lives, illustrates what is acceptable to them.

They might not say, "hey, why don't you become a

drug addict when you grow up."

Or perhaps, "why not become a fornicator or an alcoholic."

But if they themselves live such lives, they show through example what is acceptable to them.

So then, we think, "what is good enough for mom and dad is good enough for me. If such behavior is acceptable to them, then its acceptable to me."

God isn't the one who teaches us how to sin.

Parents and society teach us the patterns of destruction.

Therefore, God doesn't punish the children.

Parents punish their children by facilitating the vicious cycle that passes from one generation to the next.

All God did was warn us of the impending cycle of destruction for those who practice idolatry.

The cycle is self-propagating and facilitated by parents that simply pass on what was passed on to them.

This is an unstoppable process and a fundamental consequence of breaking the law.

God says, "if you disobey my commandments, you automatically set into motion a domino affect for three or four generations."

God says, "if you practice these things, you are not only hurting yourself but bringing potential destruction to the next three or four generations that follow."

God doesn't facilitate the problem.

We do.

The Lord simply warms us of the consequences.

By now, I'm sure you are saying, "but I don't worship idols. I don't have any statues in my home. I don't bow down to anything."

How could my life be connected to idol worship?

Idol worship isn't simply uttering some ritual on

bended knee.

It's an emotional and spiritual act as well.

Anything in our lives has the potential of becoming an idol.

Idol worship embraces many things over a wide spectrum.

It could mean bowing down and worshiping statues.

It could be a passionate pursuit of material wealth.

Idol worship is the practice of *regularly, consistently and habitually* seeking that, which brings gratification (or a high) in a time of need, hurt or anxiety, instead of seeking God first.

It's that thing we cry out for and render our will to in place of God.

Simply put, it's anything that replaces the Lord God almighty in our lives.

An idol isn't just a statue.

It's a mini-emotional god that we bond to and become dependent upon.

We yearn for it and embrace it in our hearts.

We find it almost impossible to live without.

So then, alcohol can become an idol for those who struggle with drinking, because it, not God, fills a void.

Alcoholics turn to liquor for help.

They turn to it for solace.

They seek a way to calm the voices of anxiety in their head from the daily pressures of life.

Alcohol becomes a god that brings temporary tranquility, peace and gratification in the face of screaming demons that relentlessly pursue the addicted victim.

Ultimately, alcohol replaces the Almighty God in the life of the struggling person.

Compulsive buying is perhaps the biggest worldwide vice today.

Now more than ever people are loaded down with debt, and our obsessive spending seems to be spiraling out of control.

Many people look for ways to fill the void in their lives by making purchases for items for which they have no need.

Shopping in the twentieth century has turned into a relentless pursuit of acquiring that specific article of clothing, electronic device, household appliance, new car, video game or the latest model of whatever we think will fill that empty spot in our lives.

Although it may provide a temporary high, shortly thereafter, sooner or later we return to the same sense of emptiness we had before.

We may not bow down to any physical statutes, but malls, online stores, department stores, outlet malls and market places have become places where people can worship the god of materialism.

Of course, there is nothing wrong with shopping in and of itself.

But when we habitually seek a material object to fill the void in our hearts, rather than the Lord God Almighty, it can become idolatry.

The same can be said about drugs.

More and more teenagers turn to mood altering substances that eventually create a deathly dependency.

As the dependency increases, so does the intense pursuit to "get high." The cycle accelerates until the person is physically addicted to the substance.

The body begins to demand the drug for stability.

Perhaps the drug addict doesn't bow down and worship a god called Cocaine.

Still, many are willing to kill for the substance to gain temporary relief.

Over time, it becomes their god.

Internet pornography is another area in which more and more people are becoming addicted.

This is one of the most dangerous areas, since there is hardly any exterior evidence of addiction.

Many adolescent boys are hooked on pornography before the age of 13.

Although our motor skills are not altered in the same way drugs or alcohol affect us, our mood changes as we become more aggressive in our pursuit of the high it produces in us.

Domestic violence is not exempt from being passed to the next generation.

One could make the argument that the ultimate power trip is to dominate those that are weaker or dependent.

Using violence and abuse is a means to feel in control and superior, especially during times of inadequacy and helplessness.

This, too, can become an idol.

It quenches the internal voices of anxiety and incapacity, especially as people in the home are forced to unconditionally submit.

In most cases, one parent coerces others in the household into total submission, kids and spouse alike.

How many women live with physically abusive husbands?

Their secrets go untold.

But the children are fully aware of how daddy is treating mommy.

They watch and learn their parent's behavior, and thus continue in the patterns of destruction as they begin their own families.

Food is no exception.

Many of us begin to fill our faces with food and sweets during times of anxiety.

I am not referring to eating when we are hungry.

I am talking about what psychologists call "emotional eating."

Many eat out of nervousness or anxiety.

During that time of need we can turn to a number of things.

Just look at the percentage of people in your family, neighborhood, and country who are over weight.

I must admit that I am a chocoholic.

Nothing helps me deal with the guilt I feel after eating a huge meal than devouring something really chocolaty for dessert.

Tearing down others is something people do to make themselves feel better, when they have experienced frustration, hurt or anger.

It's a way of one-upping others so that the pain, lack of fulfillment or disappointment welling up inside can be suppressed.

Bitterness, anger and hurt cause people to lash out at others.

But when these emotions go unchecked, tearing down others becomes a habit in which we find solace.

It too can become a god in our life.

Lying is a process that we use to deceive others.

Those who lie feel empowered, especially those who are compulsive liars.

They find comfort in misleading other people and have a need to manipulate the truth.

The feeling that it produces is like a high.

Thus, people turn to such a vice with regularity.

Instead of seeking truth, instead of seeking righteousness, or instead of seeking God, they seek a life of deceit.

Since a life of deception temporarily fills a void, God is replaced and idolatry sets in.

The same could be said of adultery or sexual and emotional abuse.

Perhaps excessive television is a struggle for some.

The point is that nearly anything can become an idol.

We are capable of worshiping anything imaginable.

We are capable of making anything an idol.

After looking at all of these things, it's easy for us to see how the children of those who practice these things tend to embrace them as well.

Ever hear the expression, "Chip off the old block? Like father like son?"

These phrases didn't develop out of a vacuum.

These statements developed over time, describing a simple fact: children become like their parents.

As we seek that private god in our life, a pattern of destructive behavior begins that eventually will be passed onto the next generation.

It is learned behavior.

It is branded as acceptable.

And it is taught by example by past generations.

The 60% rule

Alcoholics Anonymous says that 60% of those whose parents struggle with alcoholism will struggle with it themselves.

Although the percentage might be different for other areas yet perhaps the same could be said for those who struggle with any form of addiction.

Whether it is pornography, drug abuse, child abuse, eating disorders or any of the issues mentioned above, such behavioral patterns are learned and passed onto the next generation: the children.

Those growing up watching mom and dad smoking marijuana grow up feeling that using drugs is acceptable.

If mother and father are abusive towards each other, than most likely, the children, when they marry, will follow the same patterns.

Naturally, those who grow up being abused tend to exhibit abusive behavior as well.

Those who were sexually molested as children struggle with appropriate sexual expression and behavior.

Only time will tell what kind of pornographic addictions our society will have after several generations of constant viewing of such graphic images on the Internet.

Eating disorders and obesity are problematic as well.

Perhaps, you can envision an individual in your life that has that issue.

In most cases, one or more of their parents struggled with the same issue.

Doctors say that if one parent is overweight, the child has a 40% chance of being overweight.

If both parents are overweight, the child faces an 80% probability of being overweight.

Of course, there are exceptions.

But all in all, children learn destructive behavioral patterns from their parents, and that is how they are passed from one generation to the next.

It is a learned process.

God doesn't punish children.

Parents punish children and in most cases do so unknowingly.

Take for example a man who is a workaholic.

His children grow up watching their father's example and his extreme desire to be productive.

The price he pays will be the little time he spends with his children and wife.

He might even lose his family in the process.

What is the long-term consequence?

His children grow up with the same tendencies.

Since their father was never home and worked 80 hours a week, it must be acceptable for them to do the same in their marriages.

As a side note, if the wife feels neglected, she might reach out to another man who can make her feel appreciated, and thus several destructive patterns begin.

First, the father shows his acceptance for workaholism.

He also shows his children and his marriage that they are not as important as his career.

Further, if the wife strays, she silently suggests that adultery is permissible.

We all know, however, that it doesn't stop there.

In many cases we could easily add in drinking, yelling, abuse and violence to the mix and that might be a fair description of the average family we see around the world today.

The end result is a hostile divorce — more than 50% of marriages end in bitter court disputes.

Children are left in conflict and feel neglected and in many cases will repeat the same cycle of destruction.

A diabolic force

One other element cannot be excluded from the process.

There is a diabolical force that slithers into the mix.

After watching what half the planet saw on September 11th 2001, there is no doubt — not even in the minds of many agnostics.

Evil exists.

He is the one true enemy of God.

Given his diabolic nature, he would destroy as many lives as possible.

He leads an army that desires to obliterate our lives.

The Bible says in 1 Peter 5:8 "Be self-controlled and alert. Your enemy the devil prowls around like a roaring lion looking for someone to devour."

Satan's sole purpose is to bring destruction and death to all that God has created.

Satan uses all forms of addiction, abuse, pain, depression, hatred, anxiety and alienation to bring about the destruction of the creation of God.

He desires to break up marriages, annihilate families, weaken relationships and eradicate love and peace from the face of the earth.

In short, he desires to destroy you and me.

Therefore, he utilizes all destructive behavioral patterns to bring about our destruction and demise.

These are tools used by Satan to accomplish his objective.

How does he do this?

He throws temptation in our daily path.

He constantly bombards us with luring offers that lead us to compromise the laws that God has handed to us.

People get bombarded by many things.

To try and get us to break the first two commandments, he might use loneliness and alienation to encourage us to look for solace through substance abuse.

He could use different types of television, movies and advertisements as well as friends, family and acquaintances.

Your enemy knows your weakness.

Why tempt you in an area in which you are strong?

No.

Satan puts temptations in your path that he knows

could bring about your fall.

Let me use food as an analogy.

Have you ever been on a diet?

I think half the planet, at one time or another, has tried to lose weight.

It's sort of a painful experience, especially the first couple of days.

First you have to muster up the courage to attempt the wonderful task of lowering your caloric intake and increasing your daily activities.

Then you must find the strength and will power to be disciplined in your eating and exercise.

Let's say you start off great.

You have a week or two under your belt.

You've been exercising.

You're avoiding chocolate bars, fried foods, buttered bread and twenty-ounce frappuccinos.

All of a sudden, you get a call from a friend or family member inviting you over to his house for dinner.

You mention that you are watching what you eat.

You arrive and see that the place is well decorated.

The atmosphere is ideal for a nice friendly dinner.

They serve you chicken, knowing that you are watching your weight.

But the chicken is incredible.

So maybe you have an extra helping.

After all, it is only chicken.

Maybe you have an extra glass of that wonder fruit drink.

Maybe you have an extra helping of the cheese broccoli.

After all, it is a vegetable.

You think to yourself, "Hey I haven't done so bad thus far."

Then they bring out the dessert ... your favorite dessert.

Itŝ a chocolate-coffee mud pie made from Hägen-Dazs ice cream smothered in hot fudge sauce.

As your friend approaches the table with this monstrosity of a temptation, you notice the toasted slivered almonds that blanket the outer edges.

All of a sudden, every voice reminding you how fat you were when you started this venture has been silenced.

Your clothes do not seem to fit as tight.

You think, "hey I've got more room down there for this pleasurable experience."

Maybe I'll just have half a piece.

So you go to work very slowly on the first half.

The table talk goes on and on.

People are joyful.

The conversation is light.

No one clears the table, and you try not to stare at the remaining portions of the mud pie.

But you cannot help it.

It's as though the mud pie begins to speak to you by saying, "What a waste! I am all alone here waiting to bring someone immeasurable culinary pleasure. I am here for the taking. Come on. Don't let me go to waste."

You cannot help it.

You grab your fork and slice off a sliver from the other half that you left on the serving tray.

Besides, it was your piece.

After a minute or two passes, you shave off yet another piece.

Pretty soon you notice that you have devoured most of it.

So you finish it off.

The damage is done.

You've fallen into temptation not because of steamed

vegetables or by broiled fish.

You fell because of something that tempted you.

It was as if you were prevented from seeing the consequences of your actions.

You were hit by the one thing that was the most difficult to resist.

And as you fell, you justified your actions during the whole experience.

Now, if you add up the extra piece of chicken (250 calories), cheese broccoli (350 calories) and the mud pie (1200 calories) you'll find that you ate more in one night than you normally would in three.

The next day you stand on the scale.

That is the moment that the blinders fall and the reality sets in.

It measures you as a pound-and-a-half higher.

Your confidence diminishes.

Dieting is put on the shelf until the next time you can't stand yourself to the point of trying to do something about it.

Temptation from Satan works in similar ways.

We could substitute the mud pie for an extra marital affair or drugs or anything else that causes you to fall.

He promises pleasure, fun and excitement.

Just like the mud pie, when confronted with temptation, we cannot see how this will affect our life, marriage, children or health.

We become blinded to the consequences of our actions.

The mud pie silenced our discipline as well as the voices that told us how much we weighed and how tight our clothes were fitting.

In the same way Satan presents us with temptations that prevent us from hearing clearly the voice of reason, the voice of goodness, the voice of righteousness, the voice that helps us make healthy choices for ourselves and our loved ones.

Every time temptation leads us to break one of God's spiritual laws, we stand on the scale of life the next morning and realize the damage that has been done.

We can hear the voice of reason saying, "I tried to tell you so. But you didn't hear me."

Looking at the scale, we realize that our destructive side has gained weight.

We fed its appetite.

However, unless we learn to manage it, it will come back for more.

I am sure that by now you are asking, "How do I learn to manage my destructive behavioral patterns? How can I stop my destructive behavior?"

This is a great question.

It is the question that has led you to acquire this book.

The first step is to find the source.

How can you identify the source of your destructive behavior?

What is it that keeps you bound?

Tell me how you are feeling

Destructive patterns are not the result of an event.

They are the result of an emotion, many times an emotion centered around an event or series of events.

The event doesn't cause chaos in our hearts.

Our emotional interpretation of the event causes the craziness.

Most people who suffer with destructive habits experience anxiety, fear, hurt, resentment or some form of bitterness.

To get to the root of the emotion, you must find out how you are feeling and what has caused this emotion.

The next time you find yourself looking for whatever you are yearning to acquire, ask yourself: What am I feeling right now?

Try to isolate yourself for 10 seconds.

Find a private place.

If you cannot isolate yourself physically, then do so mentally.

Ask yourself the following questions: Do I feel secure or anxious?

Do I feel in control or hopeless?

Do I feel forgiving or angry?

Do I feel hurt?

Do I feel bitter or resentful?

Do I need a release?

If so, from what?

Find the emotional source.

Is it anxiety?

In many cases it is.

Most people who are hooked on internet pornography, cigarettes, alcohol or drugs are looking for some kind of an escape.

Escape from what?

They are not trying to escape reality but rather their emotional interpretation of reality.

They are trying to escape their anxiety.

People are constantly looking for ways to calm those voices in their head that seem to be out of control.

Thus, they turn to a mood altering experience or a mood altering substance.

The next time you think you need a drink, ask yourself: What am I feeling?

Why do I need a drink?

Then ask the Lord for help.

Ask God to help you deal with the sensation of feeling out of control.

The disciples were crossing the Sea of Galilee when a huge storm came upon them and almost sank their boat.

They were experienced fisherman.

They had seen many wicked storms in their day.

But something was different.

They were convinced that they were going to die.

Jesus happened to be asleep in the bow of the boat.

They went and woke Him.

He stood up and rebuked the storm, and peace came over the region.

Many times we need God to help us manage the thunderstorms of our emotional life.

We need God to guide us through the emotional turbulence of life until we find smooth sailing.

That's why the Bible refers to Jesus as the Prince of Peace.

Jesus offers peace to those who are in the midst of the storm.

Stressed out?

Many times we turn to alcohol or drugs because we feel stressed.

Again, the pressures of your job or financial problems are not making you drink.

It's our emotional response to these circumstances that leads us to indulge in destructive practices.

When we combine our emotional mismanagement with the fact that Satan is constantly pushing temptation in our faces, it is no wonder how confusing our lives can become.

Perhaps you feel the turbulence caused by anxiety or helplessness.

Perhaps you feel angry, bitter or resentful.

Maybe you feel hurt or rejected.

Ask yourself, "What am I looking for and why do I feel like I need it? What crazy behavior am I craving?"

Get to the bottom-line emotion.

Find out what *that* particular emotion is saying and what it wants.

Bitterness and resentment tends to want to see people hurt and thus looks for revenge.

Hurt needs to lash out, and it uses anger to do so.

Your emotions will talk to you and they will tell you exactly what they want.

That doesn't mean that you give them what they want.

Just like a good parent, you find out what your child wants.

Find out why he or she is upset.

Ask the question.

Just like a child cannot keep his mouth shut, sooner or later, you'll get an answer.

So where did that come from?

Have you ever had anyone "bite your head off?"

You ask yourself that famous question, "Wow, were did that come from?"

Getting to the source of our emotional struggles is the key to enabling God's liberating hand in your life.

Yes, God is sovereign.

Sure, He can heal us, deliver us and set us free from whatever bondage we find ourselves in, in less than a second.

However, remember what I said at the beginning of the book.

This is a partnership.

This is a joint venture between you and God.

Therefore, God will help you get to the source of the pain, anxiety, hurt, resentment, bitterness, hatred, fear or depression.

God will take you by the hand and lead you through the process of discovery and recovery.

Now, what I want you to do is think about one of those times when your life is out of control.

Think about one of those times you need a drink or some other release or escape.

Think about that moment when you say, "It's all too wonderful for me. Stop the world I want to get off."

Take a good hard look at the circumstances surrounding the event and your emotional state.

Now ask yourself, "Does this remind me of anything in my past. Does this remind me of someone who hurt me or someone who let me down? Maybe I was embarrassed as a child and never worked through it. Perhaps it was triggered by something that happened to me. Maybe I felt rejected. Perhaps I have never been able to overcome the negative self-talk that makes me feel inferior."

Most of these emotions, as I mentioned earlier, are triggered by an event or a series of events.

Events in and of themselves do not cause the chaos.

Our emotional response to these events does.

Try to think of a time when you were very anxious and had no way out.

How did you feel?

Now try to think back to a time when you remember that emotion for the first time in your life.

What were the surrounding circumstances?

How did your parents treat you?

Were you made to feel ignorant, stupid or insignificant?

Find the source!

Rewrite it!

By now, you have a clearer understanding of how your parents' behavioral patterns had a profound affect on you.

By now you have a clearer understanding of how your past has been affecting your present.

You have been able to see that those episodes of feeling out of control are tied to a specific event or series of events.

You have been able to hear the negative self talk and the feelings that come as a result of emotional mismanagement.

This is where the first step in healing is going to begin.

We are going to re-write those negative self-destructive scripts and turn them into a reflection of the love of God in your life.

The end result will be a life filled with joy and meaningful connection between you and God.

Ultimately, you will see your life change dramatically.

As we discussed earlier, the way we view the world determines our approach to negotiating it.

This is why the concept of managing our self-talk is imperative.

The way you think, the very self-talk and thought patterns you embrace every second of the day determine if you will react (defensively) or instead be proactive.

Part of changing our worldview is also changing our self-talk.

Self-talk is the very thought patterns in your head.

It is the way and tone in which you speak to yourself, silently or verbally.

Everyone has it.

No one is exempt from it.

A person that doesn't think to himself is most likely dead.

Here are some classic self-talk lines that most of us have thought at one time or another:

- That was so stupid.
- I should have never said that.
- Why do I always get there late?
- I am not as smart as the rest.
- I look fat.
- My hair is a disaster.
- How could I be so stupid?
- Everyone thinks I am dumb.
- No one really cares.
- I wonder what they're saying behind my back.
- I bet she's just using me to get what she wants.
- My heart is racing — I think I'm having a heart attack!
- No one loves me.
- If they really knew me, they wouldn't like me.
- The only reason my spouse is still with me is because he or she is fat too.

Our self-talk can be very negative.

At times, it can rise to the level of paranoia.

The goal here is not to bury it or drown it out.

The goal is to manage it and rewrite it according to God's perspective.

Thus, to answer some of these statements in our mind, one might say:

- That wasn't the best thing to say, but I will make sure I respond more appropriately in the future.
- I will ask God for wisdom to respond appropriately.
- I am not stupid or dumb.
- The only dumb question is the one that isn't asked.
- If I don't understand something, that's fine, as long

as I continue to seek the answers and the truth.

- I am going to begin to manage my time better so I can arrive on time.
- The Lord wants me to take care of my body.
- I will ask Him for the willpower.
- I will choose to lose weight, and in the meantime, I will find some clothes that make me look more slender.
- I am not alone; everyone has a bad hair day.
- Besides, God has seen me at my worst and loves me dearly.
- Actually, I am very smart.
- God made me that way, and no one is examining my intelligence.
- God cares.
- I have friends and family who care.
- Most people are afraid or paranoid of things that never happen.
- Thus, I don't need to waste my time worrying about that.

So rewrite your scripts.

Rewrite them based on the love of God for you.

Let God's self esteem for you begin to overwrite the old self-destructive patterns of self-hatred.

Take a good hard look in the mirror and tell the person you see there that God loves you.

Nothing you do will erase God's love for you, nor take away his desire to spend eternity with you.

If you could have heard God's voice at the time, what do think He would have said to you to help you through?

I'll tell you what God would say.

"Life is difficult, but my love for you endures forever." He would say that you are the *apple of his eye*.

He would say that you are worth the price that His Son

paid on the cross.

He would say that if you were the only person on earth, he still would have sent His Son to pay the price of your sin.

He would say that He yearns day and night for you to live a life more meaningful.

He would say that He deeply cares about you.

He is concerned for your wellbeing.

He sees in you a great potential to rise above the storm and soar like an eagle.

No one wants you to overcome your problems more than your Heavenly Father.

No one is more in your corner than God.

No one has faith in you like God does.

Renewing your mind renews the spirit

The greatest consequence of renewing our minds with the Word of God is that it renews our spirit as well.

Each one of us has a spirit that is intertwined with our mind and body.

In addition to being born again, it needs to be recharged and reconnected with God.

The renewing of our minds rejuvenates the spirit as well.

Therefore, as we write in our journal or take note of our innermost thoughts making them subject to Christ, our spirit becomes revitalized and reconnected with God.

Take a piece of paper and draw a line down the middle.

On the left-hand side, write down all of the negative self-talk you hear in your head during times of turmoil.

Write it down, all of it.

Don't leave anything out.

It doesn't matter how ridiculous it sounds.

Every crazy thought that you have ever dreamt, thought, or told yourself.

Write down every negative self-proclaimed thought.

Once you have finished with the left side of the paper, and you need more room, continue on the other side if necessary.

In my late teens I made a huge mistake.

I decided I was going to try to mix a little champagne with another substance, all on an empty stomach.

It hit me like a ton of bricks.

All of a sudden, I felt like I had lost my mind.

I had lost all sense of time.

It was as though I was living in a parallel universe, but I was frozen in time.

I panicked, in every sense of the word.

My tongue dropped to the very back of my throat.

My heart rate accelerated.

No matter what I tried to tell myself, I couldn't find peace.

I couldn't calm those out-of-control voices in my head.

I was convinced that I had done permanent brain damage to myself.

I had a friend drive me to the emergency room within minutes.

After the doctor saw me and chuckled under his breath, he told me how foolish it was to attempt such a thing.

After about an hour and a half, things started to settle down in my head, but something left a mark in my soul.

For the very first time in my life, I lost total control of my emotions.

Fear of losing my mind and of losing control gripped me so tightly that I couldn't breath.

Then the worst thing happened: I became afraid of being afraid.

Fear and worry are two of the worst enemies we face today.

Within about four or five weeks, I started experiencing moderate anxiety attacks.

They would come in waves.

Although I never tried to combine "the bubbly" with any other substance, I was fearful that I was going to lose my mind.

I tried listening to music, distracting myself, eating, etc.

Nothing helped.

All of this started when I opened the door to the enemy by trying to experience a high.

Interestingly enough, much of the terrible self-image that had been harbored in my life for years kicked up a whirlwind of negative self-talk that was out of control.

For so many years I had heard negative things from my parents and others close to me.

I began to hear that famous tape recorder in the back of my head telling me that I was worth nothing.

I finally went to a Christian counselor.

It was there that I discovered something about myself that I had discarded my entire life.

I was raised in a home where alcoholism and family disintegration was the norm.

I believed that would have no affect on me whatsoever.

Obviously, I was wrong.

If we have no relationship with God to restore our lives, we will be held captive to repeat the same mistakes that our parents made.

The seeds of destruction began to grow in me as well.

Yes, I knew Christ at the time.

But I made a few wrong choices that led me to escape my reality.

Little did I know, I was repeating the actions of previous generations in my family tree.

After working through some tough issues, such as reprogramming the tape in my head, the counselor gave me an excellent tool.

I discovered that God wanted to help me get past the wrong choices I had made for myself.

I discovered God's tool for re-recording that tape.

Remember, our perception is the key to the way we interact throughout life.

In addition to journaling, I took a piece of paper and wrote down every negative thought on one half.

For the first time in my life, I started to listen to my emotions for no other reason than to understand them.

Like a parent that sits down to listen to his child, I took the time every day to listen to what my emotions were trying to say to me.

Guess what I discovered.

I was feeling very lonely and very sad.

Don't misunderstand.

I was not a person who struggled with depression my entire life.

I was *feeling* lonely and sad.

Simply because we feel something doesn't make us what we feel.

You might ask, "Why were you feeling sad?"

My whole life I lived away from my father.

My mom and dad were separated when I was three and divorced when I was nine.

Further, I was feeling displeased with my progress in life.

Although I was in college and doing well, I wanted to be more successful and be in a meaningful healthy relationship.

I had none of those things.

Slowly but surely, my friends were moving away or changing.

I felt as if the world was passing me by.

On top of everything else, I had never grieved the fact that my parents were divorced.

I had never grieved all the loneliness I felt in being raised by an alcoholic mother that deeply struggled with bouts of depression.

I had never listened to how I was feeling.

I simply buried it.

I stuffed it deep down inside.

I never took the time to listen to myself.

Eventually, those feelings triggered a reaction in my spirit that left me in a state of anxiety.

Whenever we do not listen to what is happening on the inside, our mind reacts like an alarm clock.

For me, it was a rude awakening from a very frightening siren.

That state of anxiety was exactly where Satan wanted me: hopeless, faithless, fearful and hunkered down in survival mode.

Whenever we fall into the depths of despair, depression, fear or anxiety, Satan rejoices.

Anxiety is the opposite of where God wants us.

God wants us to experience peace and harmony.

He desires that we have a life full of meaning and love.

After I had emptied myself on that paper, writing down all of the internal struggles, I started to write down all the things that God says about me in the Bible on the other side of that paper.

Yes, I said, "about me."

After all, the Bible says that we are created in God's image and that we were destined to become the sons and daughters of God (Rom 9:26).

So I started to write down what God says are my attributes as a son of God.

First, God loves me and cares deeply about me.

He cares about my well-being.

I cannot do anything to impress Him or make Him love me more.

His love is solid.

It is consistent.

It is not dependant upon my actions or how I treat Him.

The Bible says that Jesus came to earth and died for my transgressions.

He died in my place.

He sees me as a worthy person, someone who has eternal worth.

If God loves me just the way I am, with blemishes and all, who I am to suggest that I am less of a person?

This is exactly how God feels about you.

He loves you.

It matters not what you have done.

It matters not how good or bad you are.

God sees you with great potential to become His son or daughter.

You have great worth, eternal value.

For that reason, He sent His son to die on a cross for you — because he sees you as being worthy of redemption.

If God would send His Son to help you 2,000 years ago, why would he leave the job half finished and not help you today?

God is faithful in completing that which he has started.

You, my friend, are no exception to that rule.

Now begin to write on the right side of that paper all of the attributes that God says He sees in you.

If nothing comes to your mind, this is what the Bible says about you:

In Zechariah 2:8 it says:

For this is what the Lord Almighty says: "After he has honored me and has sent me against the nations that have plundered you — for whoever touches you touches the **apple of his eye."**

In Deuteronomy 32:10:

In a desert land he found him, in a barren and howling waste.

He shielded him and cared for him; he guarded him as the **apple of his eye**.

Psalms 17:8:

Keep me as the **apple of your eye**; hide me in the shadow of your wings.

Deuteronomy 23:5

However, the Lord your God would not listen to Balaam but turned the curse into a blessing for you, because the Lord your **God loves you**.

John 16:27

No, **the Father himself loves you** because you have loved me and have believed that I came from God.

Psalms 139

O Lord, you have searched me and you know me.

You know when I sit and when I rise; you perceive my thoughts from afar.

You discern my going out and my lying down; you are familiar with all my ways.

Before a word is on my tongue you know it completely, O Lord.

You hem me in — behind and before; you have laid your hand upon me.

Such knowledge is too wonderful for me, too lofty for me to attain.

Where can I go from your Spirit?

Where can I flee from your presence?

If I go up to the heavens, you are there; if I make my bed in the depths, you are there.

If I rise on the wings of the dawn, if I settle on the far side of the sea, even there your hand will guide me, your right hand will hold me fast.

If I say, "Surely the darkness will hide me and the light become night around me, even the darkness will not be dark to you; the night will shine like the day, for darkness is as light to you."

For you created my inmost being; you knit me together in my mother's womb.

I praise you because I am fearfully and wonderfully made; your works are wonderful, I know that full well.

My frame was not hidden from you when I was made in the secret place.

When I was woven together in the depths of the earth, your eyes saw my unformed body.

All the days ordained for me were written in your book before one of them came to be.

How precious to me are your thoughts, O God!

How vast is the sum of them!

Were I to count them, they would outnumber the grains of sand.

When I awake, I am still with you.

If only you would slay the wicked, O God!

Away from me, you bloodthirsty men!

They speak of you with evil intent; your adversaries misuse your name.

Do I not hate those who hate you, O Lord, and abhor those who rise up against you?

I have nothing but hatred for them; I count them my enemies.

Search me, O God, and know my heart; test me and know my anxious thoughts.

See if there is any offensive way in me, and lead me in the way everlasting.

Each day read a portion of scripture and look over the attributes that God says about you.

As you dedicate a few minutes every day in listening to God's perspective on life, you will be able to take off that welder's shield and enjoy life how it was meant to be enjoyed.

Between you and God, rewrite your scripts.

Rewrite the way you think.

Re-record the tape in your head.

The Bible explicitly tells us to renew our minds.

The Apostle Paul understood the great need we have to change the tape we have in our head.

That is why he states in Romans 12:2: "Do not conform any longer to the pattern of this world, but be transformed by the **renewing** of your mind. Then you will be able to test and approve what God's will is — his good, pleasing and perfect will."

You do not have to fall into the same destructive patterns in which your parents lived.

Your future is not etched in stone.

God can change the course of your destiny.

Join forces with the Lord, and turn your back on destruction.

When your mind tells you that you are not worthy or that you are stupid or fat or less of a person, begin to recite what God says about you.

Replace the lies that Satan would have you believe with the truth that God says about you.

Read God's word.

Listen to what He says about those who love and follow Him.

As you begin to listen and absorb into your mind God's self-talk, you will notice a great transformation taking place within you.

As we close this chapter together, I would like to

emphasize the tail end of the passage of scripture we looked at earlier.

Exodus 20:6 reads:

"... but showing love to a thousand *generations* of those who love me and keep my commandments."

This is God's desire for you.

God desires to bless everyone for a thousand generations of those who love Him and keep His commandments.

Let us close this chapter together by asking God to help us renew our minds.

If you will pray and ask the Lord everyday for help, He will be faithful.

And he will help you.

If you read God's Word, study His attributes and study what He says about you, your mind will begin to be transformed.

You will never be the same, and you will see the blessings of God upon your life like you never imagined possible.

If you are not sure how to pray, maybe this example could help set the tone for you.

> **"Dear Lord, I want to have your mind, your perspective and your perception.**
>
> I want to have your heart.
>
> Once again, I ask you for forgiveness.
>
> I know that I have not lived a perfect life.
>
> But right now I turn my heart to you.
>
> I want to break free from the chains that have kept me bound and perhaps have kept my family bound for generations.
>
> I want to know your love for me.

Help me to see the root of my problem.

Help me to understand where all this confusion is stemming from.

Bring restoration to those hurts that have been unresolved for years.

As you have forgiven me for all that I have done, help me to release past hurts, resentments and bitterness.

Help me to once and for all derail those patterns within me, whether from my parents or not.

I do not want to hand down this craziness to my children or coming generations.

But rather, I want to start a process of blessing for a thousand generations of those who love you and keep Your commandments.

I receive all that you have for me, and I receive your power to change.

Guide me, help me and interact with me.

In Christ's name I pray.

Amen"

Chapter 4

Rebooting the system!

If I had a dollar for every time my computer has frozen up on me, I would be a multi-millionaire!

The cursor blinks at you but will not move.

Your first choice is to hit "Escape."

But the cursor keeps blinking.

So then you try a few other combinations that you have heard about to thaw your frozen delight.

Still, nothing works.

Then you try the grand daddy of them all.

You hit "Control, Alt, Delete."

All of a sudden, a huge siren goes off accompanied by a warning sign taking up the center part of your screen saying, "If you do that again, you will lose everything you have not saved in your life."

In other words, all the hard work you have invested in up to this point will be lost.

Still, nothing works.

It's as though your computer has decided to go on vacation, and didn't tell you.

It's like the family that takes a trip for two weeks and leaves all the lights on a timer.

The lights are on but no one is home.

Computers do that from time to time.

They get overwhelmed and decide to check out.

And no persuasion or combination of punching in a formula will change their minds.

After all is said and done, there is no choice.

Your only solution is to pull the plug in hopes of melting the frozen ice block.

Cut the power, count to ten and reboot the system!

Many times, that is what we need in life.

We need to reboot our system.

We need to reboot our family.

We need to reboot our marriage.

We need to reboot our body, mind, soul and spirit.

When we reboot our soul with God, it's called being born again.

It's a total renovation of our innermost being, connecting it with our maker: God.

Working together with the Lord, you will find the areas in your life that need to be transformed.

He will help you through the process as you reboot your system.

In this chapter, we're going to focus on rebooting your system, erasing the old thoughts and habits, and replacing them with Godly habits, such as reading the Bible, communicating with God, and gathering with other believers.

Once we have developed these habits, we can then focus our attention on managing those specific areas that have spiraled out of control and kept us in bondage.

In 1991, my mom lost her husband to cancer.

After a six-month bout, he passed away in November of that year.

My mom had become a widow and was suffering from depression.

Living in a mountain resort was very difficult, and after

losing her husband, it turned into the battle of her life.

She slipped further and further into depression, and her drinking addiction grew each day.

She had very little hope for recovery and virtually no support system or family.

At the time, my wife and I were living in Central America and found it challenging to stay in touch with her.

One night my mom had reached the end of her rope.

She called me after consuming a fair share of wine and told me that she had nothing to live for.

She said, "My husband died and made me a widow. My grandchildren no longer live in this country. I see my son once every several years. I have no job. I have no friends. I have no family."

Those words haunted me for minutes, hours, days and months.

Time passed.

Then one afternoon, her next-door neighbors invited her over for a social gathering.

After having a few drinks, eventually, the festivities winded down.

By then it was night, and she decided walk to home.

The path leading to her front porch was not lit.

There was no moonlight and no streetlights.

Everything was dark, to the point where she could not see her hand in front of her face.

As she walked up the incline to her porch, she tripped and fell face first into the jagged rocks that lay at the base of the deck in front of her home.

The fall was brutal and caused several facial bones, including her nose, to fracture.

Everything happened so fast that she was unable to lift her hands to protect her face from the blow.

Staggering to her feet with a minor concussion, she somehow made it inside the house.

She called a caring Christian friend, who began to clean her wounds and administer first aid.

Her friend offered a simple piece of advice, "Why not give God a try. Come with me to a class where you can learn about God."

The next morning my mom decided that in order for her to turn her life around, she would need to partner with God.

The most convincing sight she witnessed was her image in the mirror: a broken person with a broken life.

She prayed, "God, only you can help me turn my life around. You and I will have to make it happen."

That was the definitive moment of her life.

She hit rock bottom and had nowhere else to turn.

Without God, her life would have self-destructed.

She had become like that cursor on the computer screen, completely frozen, helpless and unable to help herself.

She came to the most important realization of all.

She needed to reboot her system.

At that moment, she desperately needed God.

She needed His sovereign embrace.

She needed Him to hold her tightly on His lap.

And in spite of all the craziness, He was there for her.

He was the only one who could carry her through the darkness.

In short, God came through.

Several months had passed and people from a

church began to reach out to her.

They invited her to church.

It was during that season in her life that the rebooting process began.

She began to read the Bible, pray and shortly thereafter attend church.

Months after her episode, we could see a noticeable difference in her demeanor.

She was still pessimistic, depressed and at times very lonely.

But God gave her the strength to stop drinking, and after several years she became an entirely different person.

To this day, she remains sober.

Years have passed since then, and she has become an entirely different person.

She regularly attends church and volunteers, sometimes several days a week.

She is a head usher and one of the most faithful lay ministers in her church.

She has served as an altar worker.

My mother has become an outstanding Christian and a caring human being.

It's been close to ten years since her severe bout with depression and alcoholism.

What made the difference?

She decided to partner with God.

Together they won the battle and have established a path blazed with the blessings of God.

Today she is a woman of God, honored and respected by her friends and family, and I am proud to say that she is my mother.

She is a perfect example of someone who was able to reboot the system and start over.

Renewing the mind

In the previous chapter we talked about the necessity of renewing our mind by re-programming the tape in our head.

That is the process of rebooting.

The best way for us to renew our minds is to read the Bible and accept what God says about us.

As we begin to think about ourselves the way that God thinks about us, a transformation begins to take place within us.

We begin to rethink the very thoughts in our head.

That is why the Bible says in 2 Corinthians 10:5 "We demolish arguments and every pretension that sets itself up against the knowledge of God, and we **take captive every thought to make it obedient to Christ**."

Every thought in our minds has to be subject to Christ.

There is a constant war being waged in our minds twenty-four hours a day, and we determine which side wins.

Will we choose destruction, the path that the enemy would have us embrace?

Or will we choose life, God's choice for our destiny?

Every thought must be placed in the light of God's plan and values in order to be examined for what it truly is.

The first habit in realizing change is to fill our head with God's thoughts.

We do this by reading the Bible.

But I hate to read

When I was a third grader, my teacher sent me to reading lab.

I was a very slow reader and couldn't retain much of what I read.

I remember having to increase the number of words I read per minute by using a teleprompter.

Only about two or three students in each class had to go to reading lab.

To say the least, I felt stupid and was always at the tail end of the class.

To this day, whenever I have to read something out loud in public, I practice several times beforehand.

My inability to read well as a child led to insecurities as a teenager and thus I hated to read.

One of the persons with the most influence on me as I began my relationship with the Lord once told me sternly, "If you want to see God change you and do great things in and through you, you must read His word! Read a chapter everyday and begin with the book of John."

So I did.

First, I bought a modern day translation of the Bible and started to read a chapter everyday.

I found what I was reading very interesting.

Many days I found myself reading two or three chapters.

Then I jumped back to the Old Testament and began to read stories of King David in 1 and 2 Samuel.

I was captivated by the adventures of this great king.

But being enthralled by wonderful Old Testament stories had another unintended consequence.

After three or four months, I noticed that I was reading much faster and covering more material in a shorter amount of time.

Not only that, I was reading with greater understanding.

I began to renew my mind and reprogram the tape in my head.

In addition, my comprehension greatly improved.

The destructive thought patterns that were once racing around in my head began to be replaced with

what God's Word says.

My self-esteem began to take on a whole new dimension.

It took on a healthy tone instead of a negative one.

My perspective was changing and my perceptions were as well.

I began to think in terms of discipline instead of recklessness;

commitment instead of indifference;

righteousness instead of wickedness;

love instead of hate;

faith instead of uncertainty;

relationship instead of animosity;

forgiveness instead of bitterness;

reassurance instead of anxiety;

and happiness instead of depression.

For the first time, I began to see myself as an individual created by God and loved by Him.

I saw myself apart from my broken family and its history plagued with problems.

Reading the Bible gave me the change of heart that I needed.

It was the reboot I was looking for.

But most importantly, it gave me the greatest breakthrough of all: reading the Bible allowed me to see myself as God sees me.

However, a reboot is only the beginning.

It's the first step.

Getting up and running is a whole other story.

As we begin to read the word, we also need to take the next step: prayer.

Praying is like getting on a

Stairmaster

Once we begin to understand what God says about us and how He speaks to us through the Bible, then we can take the next step in the process: speaking to God.

Prayer intimidates many people, because for some we have no idea what to say to the Creator of the Universe.

In many ways it's like working out, and the worst time to get on a Stairmaster is the first time!

It takes endurance and experience.

If we try to work out thirty minutes the first time we step onto a Stairmaster, we may become discouraged and give up.

It's an overwhelming task.

Instead, we need to start out at a pace we can handle.

Praying is similar.

We build up to a healthy pace.

When I was in high school just beginning my spiritual journey, I had a friend who was a bit more advanced than I was.

He had begun his relationship with God about a year before I did.

Once, he invited me over to his house to shoot some pool.

I was more than excited.

I will never forget walking into that huge three level house which had a full gymnasium, an indoor spa and a jacuzzi.

The pool table could also be converted into a ping-pong table.

It was an indoor wonderland for any teenager.

They also had a very nice stereo system with boat speakers over the hot tub.

After shooting a couple games of pool, he said, "Let's take a dip in the hot tub."

Without hesitating, I agreed.

He put on Bob Dylan's album "Saved," and we began to talk about the things of God.

He shared with me how the Lord helped him put a life of drugs behind him.

At the age of eleven, he had been smoking marijuana on a regular basis.

He would hide inside McDonald's dumpsters, waiting for workers to throw out old food.

He said that one of the most peaceful experiences he ever had was going to the cemetery with another friend.

Both would smoke a joint or two, lie down and listen to Led Zeppelin.

He said he could feel peace among the dead.

His parents tried to help him, but he didn't respond to any of their attempts.

Finally, they sent him to a drug recovery halfway house.

After a short time, he was asked to leave.

In a last ditch effort, his parents sent him from California to Minnesota to a ministry for young teenagers struggling with drugs.

It was there that he had a dynamic encounter with the Lord.

He learned the importance of prayer and reading the Bible.

The pastor guided him in a disciplined spiritual workout to gut out all the old junk that Satan had sown into his mind.

They then started implementing new habits into his life so that he would not fall back into the old patterns of destruction.

Shortly thereafter, he returned to Southern California a new young man.

Six months later, we were sitting in his hot tub.

After telling me about how God helped him through what most would call "the impossible," he turned to me and said, "Hey, why don't we pray for our high school."

It was as if the world had stopped, and I was frozen in time.

Within two seconds, my blood pressure shot up to about 150 over 95.

I had never prayed out loud before, especially in front of someone else.

"Good heavens," I thought.

"What would I say to the Creator of the Universe? He'll probably think that I stink at praying."

However, another voice took over in my head.

Which one?

The one that comes from God's word.

The Bible verses I had read, all of a sudden, took over.

I thought, "Well, all God wants from me is for me to give it my best."

So I said, "Let's go for it ... but you go first!"

He prayed with such conviction and enthusiasm.

He prayed such a dynamic prayer, raising his voice.

He seemed to know beautiful words that I am sure were pleasing to God.

He asked God to help people find the truth; to rescue those who are lost and have no hope; to help those who are suffering; to save those who were on the verge of suicide; and finally to bring about a whole new God conscious revolution in our high school.

Finally, it was my turn.

I waited for a moment of silence.

After ten seconds had passed, I said with a loud voice, "Yeah Lord! Just what he said!"

It was like getting on a treadmill or a Stairmaster for the first time.

If you haven't been on a Stairmaster or haven't worked out in a while, the first time can be exhausting and even painful.

But just like we build up endurance on a treadmill, we build up spiritual endurance as we pray and read the Bible.

And nothing will get you into spiritual shape quicker than reading your Bible and praying on a daily basis.

For me, the first time praying in that setting was intimidating and a little nerve racking.

But do you know who was more excited to hear me pray than anyone else?

Do you know who appreciated my prayer, as remedial as it was?

God.

Yes, God was proud and very pleased that I would take the time to talk with Him.

That is what God desires more than anything else from us.

He desires a relationship.

A relationship requires communication between two parties.

We listen to him, and He listens to us.

We understand Him and how he feels about us, and vice versa.

Let's kick it up a notch

Among the many wonderful things that happen when we pray, two things begin to take place.

God responds to our prayers, and we begin to be changed as a result of praying.

We hold open-air public evangelistic meetings called crusades.

We have traveled throughout Central America, the Caribbean and Mexico and have seen countless miracles such as healings, marriages restored and people set free from every type of addiction known to man.

I will never forget a young girl that came forward asking us to pray for her at the end of the first night in our first crusade.

It was a very poor town just outside of San Jose, Costa Rica called Los Cuadros.

Vivian was accompanied by her grandmother.

She was about eight at the time and missing three ribs on her left side.

She also had curvature of the spine.

Her grandmother had noticed that she was walking with a slight inclination.

So her grandmother had taken her into a medical clinic earlier that day.

The report came back after the x-rays, "We must operate on her very soon. If not, she will become an invalid."

The news was devastating.

The family had no money.

They lived in a very poor neighborhood in a very humble house.

With little or no income, getting the operation that Vivian needed would have been impossible.

God is the God who turns the impossible into the possible.

Her grandmother explained the entire situation to me.

I turned to the little girl and said, "If you let me, I would like to pray for you Vivian."

She nodded in agreement.

Afterwards, she said thanks and walked back to her place in the back of the lot.

There were about 300 others that requested prayer that night.

So for about the next hour or so, many of us on the team were praying for them.

At the very end of the night, when there were about 30 people left, I felt a tug at my coat.

It was Vivian.

She said, "I think the Lord has healed me!"

I, like most adults would have been, was a bit skeptical.

I said, "Well, we should have a doctor take a look at that."

Little did I know at the time, but the doctor that had examined Vivian that morning had also come to the crusade that night.

Vivian pointed to him and said, "That man is a doctor."

So I walked over to him and said, "Excuse me, but this young lady went into a clinic earlier this morning."

His face lit up as he said, "Yes, I examined her this morning. She is missing three ribs on her left side, and she has curvature of the spine. If we don't operate on her, she will be an invalid."

I explained all that had happened, how we prayed for her and how she was feeling.

I said, "She says that the Lord has healed her."

He said, "Well, I can examine her right now if you want. I mean, if she is healed it will be obvious."

So he lifted up her shirt and asked her to bend at the waist.

He gently moved his fingers starting at the top of the spine and looked for any obvious holes.

Then he counted by twos from the bottom of her neck to the lower part of her back.

He looked at me with both eyebrows lifted.

He said, "The girl who came into the clinic this

morning definitely had ribs missing, and we have the x-rays to show it. But the little girl standing in front of us has a perfect spine and is not missing any ribs. I guess God must have healed her."

As we pray, God responds.

The God the Bible talks about is an interactive God.

He interacts with humankind.

He responds.

He heals.

He delivers.

He saves.

And He performs miracles.

As you begin to pray for yourself and others, take note.

You will see how He responds.

You might expect the answer to come in a different way than the way it actually comes.

But all in all, God responds and answers prayer.

The second element that begins to take shape as a result of prayer has to do with what happens to us.

Our hearts begin to change.

As we draw closer to God through prayer, we become more like Him.

We begin to take on His character.

We begin to embrace His attributes: His love for others; His concern for people's safety; His heart for the poor; and His desire to help others.

These are all byproducts of prayer.

Praying not only connects us with an interactive God who touches our lives in times of need, but puts us on a divine path that allows us to take on the attributes of God.

Spending time with God helps center our off-centered lives.

No matter who you are or what your past is, prayer

will make a definitive difference in you.

I have heard it said, "Prayer changes things."

True! And the most important thing that prayer changes is you.

These days you don't have to put on your Sunday best

Much has changed around the globe since I was a teenager.

And I am not that old.

When I first started my relationship with God, going to church meant that you had to get all dressed up.

I have been in churches where the jeans were so tight that those wearing them obviously had to jump off a roof to get into them.

I've been in churches with clean people, smelly people, smart people, big people, dressed up people, dressed down (way down) people.

You name it, I've seen it in a church.

There are churches that have homosexuals, prostitutes, gangs and fornicators.

You name it.

I have seen it.

Why do we find all types of people heading to church?

Because they recognize that they need God.

Today's church is trying to implement one simple truth about the Gospel: your hearing the message is more important than the package you are wearing.

We no longer have to put on our Sunday best to go to church.

You may ask, "What is the value in going to

church?"

That is a great question, and it demands a great answer.

There is something about being in the building, hearing a Bible centered message and worshiping with other people that is great for the soul.

Besides, it is one of God's ordinances.

Exodus 20:8 says,

"Remember the Sabbath day by keeping it holy."

Hebrews 10:25 says,

"Let us not give up meeting together, as some are in the habit of doing, but let us encourage one another — and all the more as you see the Day approaching."

Aside from being an ordinance of God, attending church provides food for our soul and a connection with Him.

There are also many other benefits that come from going to church.

On June 26, 1996 Claudia Wallis and Time Magazine released an article entitled "Faith and Healing."

In the article she explores the implications of prayer and its effects on people who are sick.

She writes:

— A 1995 study at Dartmouth-Hitchcock Medical Center found that one of the best predictors of survival among 232 heart-surgery patients was the degree to which the patients said they drew comfort and strength from religious faith.

Those who did not have such faith had more than three times the death rate of those who did.

— A survey of 30 years of research on blood pressure showed that churchgoers have lower blood pressure than non-churchgoers — 5 mm lower, according to Larson, even when adjusted to account for smoking and other risk factors.

— Other studies have shown that men and women who

regularly attend church have half the risk of dying from coronary-artery disease as those who rarely go to church.

Again, smoking and socioeconomic factors were taken into account.

— A 1996 National Institute on Aging study of 4,000 elderly living at home in North Carolina found that those who attended religious services were less depressed and physically healthier than those who didn't attend or worshipped at home.

— In a study of 30 female patients recovering from hip fractures, those who regarded God as a source of strength and comfort and who attended religious services were able to walk farther upon discharge and had lower rates of depression than those who had little faith.

— Numerous studies have found lower rates of depression and anxiety-related illness among the religiously committed.

Non-churchgoers have been found to have a suicide rate four times higher than churchgoers.

Claudia Wallis — TIME MAGAZINE JUNE 26th 1996

Reading the Bible and changing your thoughts; praying and opening the communication lines with God so He can interact with you; and attending a local group of people who have similar faith — all of these are imperative.

Now let us focus our attention on managing those areas that have spiraled out of control.

I like to call it focusing on the matters that matter.

Practice common sense in all matters that matter

Let me put forth some helpful hints on how to avoid

the areas that have previously entrapped you.

Your biggest ally besides God himself is His wisdom in all matters.

The Bible says in James 1:5, "If any of you lacks wisdom, he should ask God, who gives generously to all without finding fault, and it will be given to him."

It also says in Proverbs; 14:1, "The wise woman builds her house, but with her own hands the foolish one tears hers down."

Embracing healthy habits, along with practicing common sense, will allow us to move away from those destructive patterns in our life, including relationships that tear us down and are destructive.

If you had a ten-year old daughter and a man broke into your house to rape her, would you do everything you could to protect her?

Would you throw everything at him and do whatever may be necessary to stop the intruder?

Would you call the police?

Would you yell for help?

Of course you would.

Who wouldn't?

Practice common sense.

If you would stop someone from harming your ten-year old daughter, then you ought to stop the crazy behavior and the crazy relationships that are destroying your life.

That's common sense.

If you have struggled with an addiction, disorder, abusive or compulsive behavior, there are a couple of examples of common sense and healthy practice that will help you in times of difficulty.

Focus with me for a moment on the difference between how men and women face temptation.

See no evil & feel no evil

Men and women are different in many ways.

They answer questions differently when asked.

They react differently when confronted.

They retort differently when prodded.

They respond differently when offended.

They conduct themselves differently when in public.

They reply differently when questioned.

And, of course, they behave differently when tempted.

They also manage the way they are stimulated in different ways.

When tempted, women internalize the temptation and ponder it in their emotions.

Men, when tempted, become quiet like a lion hiding in the tall grass hunting his prey.

Men are affected by what they see.

Women are affected by what they feel.

That is not to say that women are not affected by what they see or that men are not affected by what they feel.

However, on the whole, men are more likely to be stimulated through their optical sensors, whereas women are more likely to be stimulated through their feelings becoming aroused.

Men and women are wired differently and thus behave differently.

That is why many men struggle with pornography.

It is a visual stimulation that plays over and over in the movie theater of the mind.

Women struggle with unresolved emotions that fester in feelings of helplessness and depression.

They find themselves churning the emotional brew,

savoring the aroma that such emotions give off.

If you are willing to accept these basic truths about men and women, let me offer some helpful advice that I have seen work in the lives of thousands of people.

If you are a man who has struggled with pornography do not watch TV alone.

Avoid the visual sensory input that has affected you over the years.

I know a man that drapes a towel over the television every time he checks into a hotel, to avoid looking at a blank screen.

Eliminate the source of your temptation at its roots.

For men, I would say, watch out what you watch!

Try not to see (watch) any evil.

The same could be said for internet browsing.

Put filters on your computer and have someone else install a password, so that visiting questionable web sites becomes very difficult, if not impossible, for you.

If you are a woman who has struggled with bitterness, anger or depression, try not to sit alone, letting those emotions fester inside of you.

Create healthy ways to get them out.

Journaling is a great method of cleansing the soul.

Write down your emotions, every last one of them.

At times, I write them out as a prayer to the Lord.

This helps to clear them out of the head.

Then you will feel relieved from the pressure that has been building up inside.

Women who keep journals tend to be healthier and take much better care of themselves than women who do not.

Feel through the feelings so that you can manage them.

Try not to feel (and thereby cultivate) any evil.

A few nuggets of wisdom from grandma

The bottom line is to practice common sense and follow good advice.

I have no idea how wise your grandmother was, but mine raised nine children on her own.

Along the way, she picked up many great tidbits of wisdom, as most grandmothers do.

She told me how I should eat, what was good for me and when I should go to bed.

She took me to a church every Sunday morning.

I didn't understand a word, because the entire mass was in Arabic.

But the point is that she was disciplined in many important areas in life.

Even though she has passed on, I still heed her advice in many ways to this day.

The advice is easy to follow but requires determination.

If you have struggled with alcoholism, avoid establishments that serve liquor.

Try to drink water or sparkling water when at social events.

The fizz will help you feel like you are drinking something a bit more interesting than water.

If you are a drug addict, begin to be selective about the friends you spend time with.

In most, if not all cases, it would be best to cut off all drug-related relationships.

If you are an overeater, portion out your food.

Weigh it out ahead of time and store away the rest until the next day.

Try not to shop when you are hungry.

When possible, plan ahead by taking your food with you on the road.

If you get anxious, separate yourself from food during times of anxiety.

Most overeaters that consume food do so not for hunger, but for emotional reasons.

If you are a workaholic, try not to take work home.

Give yourself permission to relax at the end of the day.

Spend time resting and relaxing, and try to close those work related doors.

Further, your body needs to recuperate.

Thus, you shouldn't feel guilty for sleeping eight hours a night.

If materialism is driving you to overspend, allow someone else to handle the finances.

Make sure that person is responsible and trustworthy.

Leave your wallet in the car, for example, when shopping in a mall.

When you are tempted to make a purchase, having to walk back to the car provides extra time for common sense to kick in.

Finally, I cannot overstate the importance of eating right and exercising.

Most people fall short of their potential simply because they cannot control their culinary temptations.

Many people around the world are compulsive eaters.

Most people in the world are overweight.

Probably 30 percent are dangerously overweight.

We are not getting any better, unfortunately.

We seem to be getting fatter and fatter.

This causes an unbalance in our system, which creates huge mood swings, lowers energy and increases sickness.

Needless to say, all of that costs you money in doctor's bills, down time and simply put, increases the "I need to get away from it all" feeling.

So do what your grandmother told you to do.

Eat all your vegetables.

Eat lots of fresh fruit.

Try to stay away from fried foods.

High concentrations of sugar, fat, cholesterol, sodium and simple starches can be dangerous.

Managing the way you eat will help your moods stay at an even keel.

If you don't feel depressed, then you'll be less likely to fill the void in your life with food.

Let me elaborate a bit more on this issue, an issue that so many of us struggle with.

The Bible, in 1 Corinthians 6:19 & 20, says, "Do you not know that your body is a temple of the Holy Spirit, who is in you, whom you have received from God? You are not your own; you were bought at a price. Therefore honor God with your body."

Imagine for a moment that you purchase a brand new bright red Ferrari.

It has twelve cylinders, is fuel injected and is imported directly from Italy.

The lettering is in gold, twenty-four karat.

The seats are made from genuine leather.

The doors open out and upward over the top of the vehicle.

It has well over 400 horsepower, and it has six gears.

Let's say that you paid close to $300,000 for the car.

The insurance premiums are over $15,000 per year, and you've installed "LoJack," the anti-theft car protection monitoring system.

You love your car so much that you've placed an additional home security system in the garage just to make sure it is double protected.

When you sit in the driver's seat, you relish that new car-leather smell.

The dash has no dust particles on it whatsoever.

The stereo system is a Blapunk with eight perfectly positioned speakers for optimal listening.

It can play CDs, MP3s and has a satellite hookup so you can listen to over 150 radio stations of every style of music available.

The seat is contoured to fit your back.

It seems to hold you in its lumbar arms.

You think to yourself, "This car was made just for me."

In the first month, it seems as though you wash and wax the car everyday.

You change the oil, oil filter and air filter once a week.

You don't let anyone who smokes or eats come within 100 feet of the vehicle.

People have to take off their shoes just to sit in the car.

Over time, something begins to change.

You stop changing the oil once a week.

You stop washing it once a day.

Eventually, you stop buying the highest-octane fuel.

Washing the car becomes a thing of the past.

You start putting in regular unleaded gasoline.

You stop taking it for a spin.

Until finally, you decide that you do not want to spend any time going to the gas station.

Instead, you take a ten gallon bucket and put some coffee, alcohol and some sugar in, mixing it all together before pouring it into the tank.

If the car starts, it is very unlikely that you will be able to get it out of the garage.

That would be a miracle.

The car won't run, and it has lost its functionality.

Think about it for a moment.

You have the fastest, most seductive vehicle on the face of the planet.

And you are pouring sugar and coffee into the tank.

You might say, who in the world would do that?

No one would do that.

No one in his or her right mind would do such a thing ... except when it comes to our bodies.

In that case, most people treat their bodies just like that.

They pour hundreds of pounds of sugar and fat into their bodies.

The human body and the human mind are far more superior to any creation that man has conjured up.

The body is the finest architectural creation that God has designed.

Yet we treat that structural wonder as if it were a trashcan.

An interesting statistic came out yesterday.

Americans eat over 155 pounds of sugar each year.

That is twice as much as what our grandparents used to consume.

We seem to be dumping pounds of fat, sugar and toxins into our bodies on a monthly basis.

We never exercise it; never take it out for a spin; never clean out the valves.

In most cases the most exercise we do is going from the couch to the refrigerator and back again to eat more junk.

The point here is clear.

Treat your body better than you would a brand new Ferrari.

It's worth much more.

It will outperform, outthink, and outlast a Ferrari any day of the week, as long as you treat it right.

In doing so, you will notice that the battles you face on every front are much easier to fight.

You might ask, "So what do I do?"

The most important thing you can do is consult a physician.

What I am saying does not apply to everyone.

Everyone's body is different, and what worked for me might not work for you.

Once you have talked with your doctor to determine a healthy menu and exercise program, begin slowly.

Now as a guideline, I will share what worked for me.

First, find a weight that the doctor (not your friends) says would be adequate for you.

Do not depend on close friends to tell you whether or not 150 or 250 pounds represents the ideal weight for you.

Ask a doctor, and get an objective opinion.

Use that as a goal.

I started by exercising at least five times a week in thirty-minute segments.

I started with a brisk walk and as my endurance increased, I transitioned into a walk/jog routine.

Monday through Friday, I walked and ran in intervals of two minutes for a total exercise time of thirty minutes.

I then added weightlifting to my routine, for about fifteen to twenty minutes, Monday through Friday.

Dumbbells were sufficient for me.

Heavy weightlifting was not necessary.

Second, I drank about three quarts of filtered water everyday.

Skim milk serves as an excellent balance between

carbohydrates and protein.

I drink about a glass or two a day.

I try to stay away from sodas and caffeinated products.

Occasionally, I have a cup of Costa Rican java, but I try not to make a daily habit out of it.

Finally, I stay away from simple starches, if possible.

I try to eat as much fresh fruit and vegetables as possible, especially broccoli and cauliflower.

I have tried to eliminate fried foods as well as products high in saturated fat.

For protein, I eat about six egg whites each day for breakfast and six ounces of boiled chicken for dinner.

I might have a can of tuna for lunch.

As a result, I feel much better and have much more energy than I previously had.

Dream it

Imagine a life where you wake up in the morning feeling like you have slept for eight-and-a-half uninterrupted hours.

You don't feel dehydrated or hung-over.

You feel refreshed.

You get up excited to face your day.

You look into the mirror and like what you see.

You think to yourself, "God loves me, and I am so privileged to live the life I live. I wouldn't trade my life for anyone else or for all the money in the world. God is pleased with me."

In order for you to say that, you need to have peace and be at peace.

You need to be at peace with yourself and with God.

I have traveled the world and I can testify of what the world is searching for.

People want peace.

People want harmony.

More than anything, they want a divine connection with God.

You are looking for what six billion people are looking for.

And you will find it as you put into practice everything we have discussed in the previous pages.

As you read His word, God's peace begins to permeate your mind.

You reprogram the tape in your head and begin to see things from God's perspective.

You begin to take on God's perception.

In pursuit of God's peace, you take an additional step.

You begin to dialog with Him on a daily basis.

This is what we call prayer.

In any relationship, communication is the cornerstone.

Prayer is our way of communicating with God, thus strengthening our relationship with Him.

Then tie in to a local body of believers.

This acts as a way to feed your soul and share with others of like faith.

In addition, actively attending a local church has greater implications that affect your overall life and health.

Studies have shown that people who adhere to faith in God and attend local churches on a regular basis are much more likely to live healthy and flourishing lives.

In cases where they are sick, their recovery rate far exceeds those who have no church affiliation.

Finally, do not underestimate the importance of taking good care of your body.

It is the only one you have, and in this lifetime, you only get one.

Treat it better than a brand new house or sports car.

If you take good care of your body, it will take good care of you.

By now, I think that you've caught onto a good habit that I am trying to pass onto you.

I have ended each chapter with a closing prayer.

I do that in case you have never prayed and need a guide.

In any case, this is what I leave with you as you attempt one of the most difficult steps, implementing good habits and replacing destructive ones:

"Lord, I thank You for another day of life.

I recognize that without You, I have no life.

Jesus, you are the source of life, and I ask You for the opportunity to reboot my system.

I need to restart my life.

I want to be born again.

Forgive me for any sins hidden or exposed.

I accept You as my Savior and Lord.

Help me read Your Word.

Show me new insights and help me to understand it.

Put people in my life that will help me to understand Your Word as it was meant to be understood.

I also ask You to help me pray.

Help me to always turn to You in my time of need, opening the lines of communication so that I do not sink into depression or loneliness.

Lead me to a church and help me to become involved so that I can learn more about You and establish meaningful relationships.

And help me move away from those relationships that are destructive and harmful to me.

Finally, I ask You to remove me from temptation.

Deliver me from those things that are enticing and harmful.

Above all Lord, deliver me from evil.

I ask these things in Christ's name, Amen."

Chapter 5

Let the dead bury the dead

When I was six, my mom took me to buy some ice cream.

It was about 7:00 PM and a beautiful Southern California summer night.

I was so excited.

There's nothing better than when your mom or dad says, "Come on. Let's go get some ice cream."

I remember driving into the parking lot of the Sav-On Drug store in Calabasas, which is in the West end of the San Fernando Valley.

My mom parked her 1969 Volkswagen bug and started to dig into her hippy-style leather purse, scrounging around for thirty cents.

In those days that was all it cost for two double ice cream cones.

She sent me into the drug store with the money, and I repeated over and over in my head the combination of ice cream flavors she wanted.

I wanted to show her that I could pay for her ice cream and pick out the right flavors.

"I am a big boy now," I thought. "I can do it all by myself."

The clerk leaned over the top of the refrigerated ice cream storage bin, which was made of glass, and said, "Can

I help you?"

I said, "Yeah, I'll take one cone with Rocky Road and Mint n' Chip. I'll take another cone with Pistachio and Coffee."

"Will that be all?" he asked.

"That will be all," I replied.

I waited patiently for both ice cream cones.

I knew that I had to pay and hurry back to the car or the ice cream would begin to melt.

I handed him a quarter and a nickel.

He handed me the two cones, and I stepped onto the mat that opened the electric door for me.

Of course, as child I couldn't wait to give my cone a lick.

Thus, while walking across the parking lot, I made a grave mistake.

I started on my cone before I got back to the car.

It is hard to do two things at once, especially walking, eating ice cream and balancing your mother's cone in an upright position.

While I was sculpturing my cone in the shape of a tornado whirlwind, I failed to notice that my mom's cone was leaning to the left at a forty-five degree angle.

When I finally realized what was happening, the Leaning Tower of Pisa began to fall.

It dropped from the cone in slow motion, toppling end over end, until finally it splatted right smack in the middle of a parking stall.

Perhaps "grease slick" would be a better way of describing where my mom's ice cream met its doom.

Now keep in mind that for a young boy six years of age, ice cream on the ground is just as good as ice cream still on the cone.

Being a good boy, I bent down, scrapped up the ice cream, slapped it back on the cone and headed back to the car.

My mom looked so excited to see her favorite flavors towering over a large sugar cone.

She said, "You did it."

I beamed with pride and jumped in the back seat.

She started in on hers in the front seat.

After about the second lick, I watched her through the rear view mirror.

I noticed her pulling something off of her tongue.

She mumbled to herself, "What? What is this? Is this glass?" with a shocked look on her face.

After pulling it off of her tongue, she quietly wiped it on a napkin.

The very next lick, her eyebrows frowned severely as she said, "There is a hair in my mouth ... and this ice cream tastes like motor oil."

Finally, she asked me, "Jason, did something happen to my ice cream?"

I said, "No. Your ice cream is fine."

Then she said, "Then why does it taste like motor oil? Jason, did you drop my ice cream?"

I said nonchalantly, "Yeah, but then I picked it up and put it on the cone so you could eat it."

At that moment, my mom had to make a very important decision.

Would she harbor feelings of anger?

Or would she forgive her son?

To this day, we laugh about my desire to hide a mistake.

Had her ice cream fallen into something toxic, the story could have ended much differently.

Imagine if that broken glass had gotten wedged in her throat.

She could have been seriously injured, and she might have held it over my head for years.

She could have become angry about this.

But she didn't.

My mom chose to forgive me.

She did not let the sun go down on her anger.

She didn't carry a grudge.

She decided to let it go.

Some people may have exploded at their children for doing such a brainless thing.

Instead, my mom chose the high road.

Close the door to Satan

The Bible says in Ephesians 4:26 & 27: "In your anger do not sin. Do not let the sun go down while you are still angry, and do not give the devil a foothold."

Something happens within us when we do not release our anger and forgive others who have hurt us.

Going to sleep (allowing the sun to go down while we are still angry), allows us to forget about what happened but not forgive what happened.

The next day we may feel refreshed, and we may not feel angry at all until we are reminded of our emotional injury.

But the anger has festered within us and continued to grow like a fungus.

When we are reminded of what happened, it's like a scab that is ripped off, exposing the wound once again.

A person who cannot forgive is someone who becomes a negative and pessimistic individual.

He or she finds it difficult to trust others and nearly impossible to live a meaningful life full of joy.

That is why the Bible exhorts us to not give the devil a foothold.

Do not give him any area of your life.

Do not be angry.

Living in anger only destroys you and allows Satan to have dominion over your life.

The anger we see in the Middle East, for example, is fueled by hatred caused by hurts.

These hurts started thousands of years ago and have continued through the centuries.

Still, for several millennia, that part of the world has let the sun go down on extreme anger.

Simply put, because of a lack of forgiveness, both sides suffer to this day.

Forgiveness is the only solution for the world conflicts we see today.

Forgiveness, for most of society, is not something that is given much attention.

It's an issue largely overlooked in our day.

Jesus understood the power of forgiveness.

To him, forgiving others was imperative for a meaningful and significant life.

This was so important to Him that our being forgiven was made contingent on us forgiving others.

In Luke 11, Jesus teaches His disciples a famous prayer still used by hundreds of millions of people today.

He said to them, "When you pray, say: 'Father, hallowed be your name, your kingdom come. Give us each day our daily bread. Forgive us our sins, for we also forgive everyone who sins against us. And lead us not into temptation.'"

This prayer has been called the "Our Father."

These words are repeated almost on a weekly basis in Christian churches all over the world.

Why?

It contains the necessary elements for a good prayer.

It contains worship, it seeks God's will, and it petitions for basic needs.

Notice that twenty-five percent of the prayer is dedicated to forgiveness.

He stresses the need for us to ask for forgiveness every day.

It should be a normal part of our prayer life.

Married to that notion is the concept of forgiving others.

We often hear about the importance of asking God for forgiveness.

However we rarely hear any teachings about forgiving others.

Jesus says in verse four, "Forgive us our sins."

Here, he uses four words emphasizing our need to ask God to forgive us.

These four words are followed by a comma, then a declaration: "for we also forgive everyone who sins against us."

We are not asking God to forgive other people's sins against us.

This is not a petition.

It's a statement.

As we pray, we ask God for forgiveness, because we too are actively forgiving others.

How many times?

The act of forgiveness is imperative in our relationship with God.

Why?

Simply put, He forgave us.

The entire structure of our relationship with God is based upon forgiveness.

The big picture: if there is going to be harmony in God's system of life, forgiveness has to be the international language and common denominator we all speak and understand.

If forgiveness is only implemented by a fraction of those in the world, the system breaks down.

God initiated it.

He said, "I will forgive man for all that he has done: sexual immorality (adultery and fornication), impurity and debauchery; idolatry and witchcraft; hatred, discord, jealousy, fits of rage, selfish ambition, dissensions, factions and envy; drunkenness and orgies."

God has forgiven us for all of these acts.

The only condition, aside from asking God for forgiveness, is for us to forgive others as He has forgiven us.

And if we ask ourselves how many times we ought to forgive, Jesus is very clear.

To Him the number is not as important as the attitude we have in habitually extending forgiveness to others:

Then Peter came to Jesus and asked, "Lord, how many times shall I forgive my brother when he sins against me? Up to seven times?"

Jesus answered, "I tell you, not seven times, but seventy-seven times.

'Therefore, the kingdom of heaven is like a king who wanted to settle accounts with his servants.

As he began the settlement, a man who owed him ten thousand talents was brought to him.

Since he was not able to pay, the master ordered that he and his wife and his children and all that he had be sold to repay the debt.

The servant fell on his knees before him.

'Be patient with me,' he begged, 'and I will pay back everything.' The servant's master took pity on him, cancelled the debt and let him go.

But when that servant went out, he found one of his fellow servants who owed him a hundred denarii.

He grabbed him and began to choke him.

'Pay back what you owe me!' he demanded.

His fellow servant fell to his knees and begged him, 'Be patient with me, and I will pay you back.'

But he refused.

Instead, he went off and had the man thrown into prison until he could pay the debt.

When the other servants saw what had happened, they were greatly distressed and went and told their master everything that had happened.

Then the master called the servant in.

'You wicked servant,' he said, 'I cancelled all that debt of yours because you begged me to.

Shouldn't you have had mercy on your fellow-servant just as I had on you?'

In anger his master turned him over to the jailers to be tortured, until he should pay back all he owed.'

This is how my heavenly Father will treat each of you unless you forgive your brother from your heart."

Matthew 18:21-35.

Before we continue, it is important to briefly mention that if you are in a situation where you are in danger either emotionally or physically, you need to protect yourself and remove yourself from harm's way.

You can forgive someone without continuing to stay at risk in a damaging relationship with that person.

Just because we forgive someone doesn't mean that we continue to allow him or her to continuously inflict pain upon us.

We must remove ourselves from the situation or find a remedy that provides us with solace or safety.

Bring me the check

For most of us, we like the idea of being forgiven.

Especially when it comes to debts.

Wouldn't it be great if you received a letter from VISA that stated: "All of your charges are cleared. You don't owe a dime."

That would be historic.

The notion of being cleared of all charges is a great one.

That is why forgiveness of sins is so important to the spirit and the soul.

A few years back, I was about an hour early for an appointment.

I pulled off the freeway and parked in a parking structure in one of the malls in Southern California.

Before long, I fell asleep.

Several hours had passed, and it was about two o'clock.

When I woke up, I was completely disoriented.

I had missed my appointment.

I stumbled out of the car and headed across the parking lot to a restaurant called Bennigan's.

The friendly hostess greeted me at the door and asked me how many were in my party.

Not being in my right mind, I looked over my shoulder didn't see anyone else and said, "Just one, I guess."

She sat me down in a booth by the window and handed me a menu.

The bright sunlight came through, which forced me to squint for a minute or two.

After all, I had been asleep for several hours, and my eyes had not adjusted to the sun.

Turning my head away from the window I opened the menu and looked for the dish that had the most amount of food.

I was looking for sheer volume.

Needless to say, I was starving.

When the waitress came to take my order, I asked her which was the biggest plate of food they had.

She said, "You should order the beef, chicken and pork salad in a shell."

I said, "I'll take it."

I also ordered a large coke and then waited anxiously for my feast.

A few minutes passed and she emerged from the kitchen doors bringing the most beautiful culinary creation I had seen in some time.

It looked like a mountain of steaming sizzling meat and chicken laid upon a bed of lettuce and refried beans.

At the base of the volcano there was a thick layer of sour cream.

Everything was resting in a huge nest, the largest tortilla shell I had ever seen.

To top it all off, they had sprinkled cheddar and mozzarella cheese that draped over the meat like snow covering the Rockies in February.

I thanked the Lord for the food and dug in.

It was such a delight.

The waitress returned about five minutes into my adventure and asked if I needed anything else.

I said that everything was fine.

When she walked away, I thought for a moment that I had everything I needed.

That was, until I remembered I had no money.

I woke up at that moment and realized that I was completely broke.

I had no credit cards with me, no cash and in those days, no one had cellular phones.

When I was a teenager, I remember working in a restaurant.

One time a couple came in and couldn't pay the bill.

The manager placed them under citizen's arrest.

As I sat there without any money, thoughts began to race through my head.

I thought, "This waitress is going to arrest me too."

Although I was distraught over how I was going to pay the bill, I still continued to eat.

Ironic, isn't it?

You know you're in trouble, yet you keep doing the things that will push you further into trouble.

When I had finished about seventy-five percent of the food, I felt conflicted.

Suddenly, I looked down and spotted something.

I thought, "That doesn't look right. That shouldn't be there."

It definitely stood out.

There it was, lying on top of one of the pieces of lettuce: a tiny hair.

At that moment, the waitress returned and said, "How's everything?"

I replied, "Everything is great. Except for the fact that there is a tiny hair right here," as I pointed to it.

She looked at me with great horror in her eyes and said, "Oh my goodness! That's terrible! I will take care of this right away!"

She grabbed the plate and rushed through the kitchen doors.

I heard some yelling on her behalf, and finally a plate slammed down on one of the kitchen counters.

After about three minutes, she reappeared and said to

me, "I am so sorry. We really want to make this up to you. What do you want in place of your beef, chicken and pork salad?"

At that point I had eaten most of my meal, and I really wasn't hungry, so I looked at her and said, "The truth of the matter is that I no longer have an appetite."

"Are you sure?" She said.

"I'm positive," I replied.

She turned around and headed back to the kitchen.

Five long minutes passed, and she reemerged and said, "Well sir, for such a disgraceful thing, we have decided to comp your meal."

"Excuse me?"

She said, "The restaurant has decided to cover the cost of your meal."

I said, "No! No! That is not necessary. I insist on paying."

Like I had any bargaining leverage.

She said, "I am sorry sir, but the manager has already 'comped' your meal. You cannot pay the bill because the restaurant has already paid it. Even if you wanted to, it would be impossible. Besides, it would throw our accounting system into a worse mess. Once the bill has been paid, you cannot repay it."

My bill had been paid.

My debt had been forgiven.

The restaurant had cleared me of all charges.

I walked out of the restaurant a free man.

When Jesus forgives us of our sins that is exactly what it means to be free.

He paid a debt upon our life that we are not capable of paying.

Only Jesus can clear us of the charges.

If you have never asked the Lord for forgiveness, now

is the perfect time to do it.

Imagine the entire load you carry suddenly being lifted off your shoulders.

Imagine the burden that you have carried for years no longer oppressing you.

Asking forgiveness from God is simple, and you will be surprised how you will feel after all of your charges with the Lord have been cleared.

Cut the ties and move on

The sense of being forgiven is a great feeling.

It is something that we love to experience.

But when it comes to forgiving others, we face an entirely different challenge.

Have you ever been fishing in a lake or river and had your bait get stuck?

So you jerk and pull on the line.

You tug up and down.

Nothing works.

If the hook is caught on something at the bottom, your only solution is to cut the fishing line.

If you don't, you might spend the whole day trying to untangle the line and thus lose the entire day in the battle.

The same is true about our lives.

When we do not forgive others, we are tied to them, like a fishing line hooked to something at the bottom of the lake.

No matter how hard we try to forget, break away, or distract ourselves, we simply drive the hook deeper into the wound.

Trying to forget about it is simply living in denial.

Eventually the wound becomes dangerously infected.

Many times, we think that we have moved past our

hurts.

But when we are reminded of the person who hurt us, it's like a scab that is ripped off.

It uncovers the very same wound and infection we had before.

In many cases, it's worse than before.

It has had time to fester.

After a crusade in March of 2003, I met with the ushers, who asked me to pray for them individually.

I was more than happy to, since they had served faithfully for one week, helping thousands of others in their community during the event.

As our team was breaking down the sound and lighting systems, I began to ask each usher how I might pray for them specifically.

It was dark in our tent, which holds about 5,000 people.

I moved through the line and came upon a woman who had her eyes closed.

As soon as I was in front of her, she shrieked a bloodcurdling scream.

My heart stopped.

With her eyes closed she took a swipe at me and yelled, "Don't let the cursed one touch me!"

She dropped to the ground covering her ears screaming: "No! No!"

She was carried by several ushers to a separate location, where we could adequately attend to her needs.

When she finally came to her senses, she confessed her life to us.

Her father had put her into prostitution as a young girl.

Living a life of drugs and abuse in a marginalized community, she learned to hate men.

She had been raped countless times.

Two weeks before the crusade, she went to a church.

The pastor was announcing that we were having an event and that we needed workers.

So she raised her hand as a volunteer.

Although she volunteered as an usher, she had never asked the Lord forgiveness; had never made a commitment to the Lord with her life; and obviously had never forgiven those who had hurt her.

All the wounds, abuse and emotional damage had led her to give her life over to hatred and bitterness.

Satan had taken parts of her life and will.

When she started to help at the crusade, she was confronted with the reality of being forgiven and needing to forgive others.

When I approached her, she began to feel very uncomfortable.

The anger inside of her exploded and she lost all control.

Satan manifested his work in her.

It was like a scab that being ripped off her body once again.

But this time it was causing severe emotional and spiritual bleeding.

The pain from her infectious bitterness caused her to snap.

Later on, in counseling her, we discovered that I was just one more man who made her feel uncomfortable.

I represented that which she hated.

My presence, as a man of authority, had caused her to lash out.

Our counselors stressed to her the importance of forgiveness.

Forgiveness is the cornerstone of a life of freedom.

It allows us to break free from those who have hurt us

and it releases us from the bonds that keep us tied to them.

This young lady began to audibly pronounce the name of each and every man that had hurt, raped and abused her.

She said his name and said, "I forgive you for ..."

Finally, she approached the most difficult bridge of all.

She had to forgive her very own father, the one who had forced her into prostitution as a little girl.

Once she made that breakthrough, those diabolic voices pounding away in her head disappeared.

A huge load was lifted off of her, and she began to experience a newfound freedom.

Doctors tell us that many heart attacks and strokes are caused by people bottling up their anger and bitterness, leaving conflict unresolved.

Doctors also tell us that many modern day diseases are the result of stress related issues.

From experience, I can say that 70% of those who come to us for help with physical, emotional or spiritual ailments have a person in their lives that they have not forgiven.

If you desire the power to change; if you want to see your life change dramatically, you must learn to forgive.

Learning to forgive will launch you into a whole new dimension.

Failing to forgive initiates a process in which you become more and more embedded with those who hurt you.

There is something ironic about not forgiving someone.

When we refuse to forgive, we stay connected to the person that hurt us.

We are linked to him or her.

The wounds and hurts we hold onto keep us bound to the person, both emotionally and spiritually.

Forgiveness is not just releasing the person that hurt us, it is releasing us from the person.

Forgiveness is the act that leads us out of a painful and hurtful destructive pattern.

The challenge

Perhaps by now you are convinced of the necessity of releasing your past hurts.

Perhaps you can now say, "I can see the need to be freed from all the bitterness I have been harboring."

After all, bitterness is the poison we drink wishing that someone else will die.

Perhaps you are ready to say, "I am tired of drinking this poison and paying the consequences for it."

Still, one difficult challenge remains: forgiving those who do not want to be forgiven.

When my first daughter was born, in October of 1990, we lived on the Vanguard University trailer park campus.

I was finishing my Master's degree, and it was an economical place to live.

Normally it gets fairly warm in Southern California for a week or two in October.

A tree was growing up against our back window, and of course, we had to sleep with it open.

This particular trailer had no screens in the windows to keep the insects out.

One night, a huge bug crawled across my forehead and woke me up.

"That's it," I thought. "We need to trim that tree. Not only is it a refuge for bugs, it's a fire hazard too."

The next day, I told the maintenance department about the problem.

They said to me, "We are short on staff. It will take about a week until we can get to it. Or if you want to trim it yourself, you've got our permission."

That was the solution I chose.

I grabbed a hacksaw and started to trim.

I probably took off too much.

But I thought that it wouldn't matter.

We were heading into the winter months, and the shade wouldn't be that important.

Two days passed, and three people came to our door.

They said, "We have a very serious situation, and we need to talk."

I invited them in.

By the expressions on their faces, I knew that they were irate about something.

As it turned out, they were our next-door neighbors and had paid to have their trailer moved and positioned next to ours.

Why?

For the shade of a tree.

Which tree?

The one I had trimmed.

I calmly tried to explain that we were having problems with the bugs, and for us, it was a fire hazard.

For them, it was a source of shade for their bedroom window.

One man's blessing was another man's curse.

So I apologized and said, "I really had no idea that my actions were causing you so much grief."

The husband replied, "Forgiveness is one thing, but restitution is another. We want you to make up the difference."

I was short of words.

I had no idea how to solve the problem.

The only thing that would apparently satisfy them was to have another tree transplanted to replace the now leafless stem coming out of the ground.

I said, "I would like to help you, but that would cost a fortune."

"We calculate that this is going to cost you at least several hundred dollars," they said.

I replied, "We're going to have to find another solution because that is completely unreasonable."

"I had permission to trim the tree," I noted.

They said, "We're taking it to the University administrator," which they did.

When they left, I was extremely upset.

I was hurt.

Not only had they ganged up on me, they had refused to consider our situation.

I had apologized to them and tried to reach out to them.

But I had been completely rejected.

After meeting with the administrator, they discovered that I had obtained permission to trim the tree.

Although the trim wasn't the greatest, nonetheless, I still had permission.

I was in no way, shape or form responsible either legally or morally to resolve the situation — the university was.

When I heard that the university was not faulting me for the incident, I went back to the couple and said, "I am still dedicated to finding a solution for you."

So after talking for about fort-five minutes, we came to the conclusion that the most important issue was for them to recover their shade in the afternoon.

So I paid for the materials for a carpenter to build a small awning over their window.

One of the maintenance personnel was installing the

awning.

The husband came out and said, "Man alive that is small."

I said, "That is what it will take to cover the window."

"No," he said. "We wanted not just the window covered, but the whole back portion of the trailer."

Finally I said, "I am paying for this out of my own pocket."

He said, "Oh big deal. How much did it cost you ... twenty bucks?"

I said, "Take it or leave it. But this conversation is over. And never bug me with your petty shade issues again."

Once again, I was extremely upset.

For the longest time, whenever I saw their car, whenever I saw their trailer, or whenever I saw their faces from a distance, it was like a scab being ripped off, exposing my wound once again.

Forgiveness is not an emotion, it's a choice

I had to make a choice.

I had to make a very difficult decision.

How do you forgive someone who doesn't want to be forgiven?

There is a seeming injustice when one feels obligated to forgive someone who could not care less about receiving forgiveness.

Still, extending the hand of forgiveness is not only God's plan for those who receive it but also for those who offer it.

I came to a point where I had to say to myself, "I

choose to forgive them."

My forgiveness for them depends not on their desire to receive it.

It depends exclusively on me and no one else.

Forgiveness is a choice, not an emotion.

I decided to forgive them.

I made an important decision.

Every time I thought of that family or saw their house or vehicle, I said to myself, "I forgave them, and I have released them from my anger."

I understand that talking about trees being trimmed and neighbors becoming angry over shade doesn't amount to much when you compare it to people being lied to, being taken advantage of, or being abused, raped or murdered.

However, the concept of forgiveness applies to all of the above.

Remember, it not only releases the offender, but it heals the offended.

How do we forgive those who are not aware that they have hurt us?

As I mentioned before, I grew up in a crazy home.

I jokingly use that term.

But when faced with the reality of having to forgive my mother for things said or for emotional abuse that was entirely unwarranted, I had to forgive her.

Remember the time I had been told to get out of the house?

The next day, she didn't remembered what had happened.

It was frustrating trying to connect with her and

reconcile what had happened.

She was completely unaware.

So what do you do in a similar circumstance?

This leads us to the second challenge in forgiveness, forgiving someone who doesn't know they have hurt you.

The principles of forgiveness are the same whether the offender seeks forgiveness or not.

I am sure that I have offended people without intending to do so.

Afterward, I probably had no idea of my offense.

In the case where my offense was innocent, I can only hope that people will have found it in their hearts to forgive me.

Where a relative or someone close has unintentionally hurt you, forgiving them is the only correct response.

If you cannot find it within yourself to forgive, your perceptions of them begin to change significantly.

You might begin to say, "What a clueless person. They are blind to the world around them."

Or perhaps, "Can you imagine having to live with someone like that? What an idiot!"

Soon we begin tearing the person down, as we seethe inside with bitterness and anger.

This starts a whole new cycle of self-destruction.

Eventually we become hooked on tearing others down with our bitter and angry spirit.

Remember, bitterness is the poison we drink hoping the other person will die.

Bitterness and anger paralyze us.

Anger strangles our ability to be fruitful in life.

Learning to manage our anger and dealing with festering emotions is one of the most important keys to developing a power to change.

How many women could become so much more, if they only learned to let the dead bury the dead and forgive those who have trespassed against them?

How many men would have developed great careers, had they learn to forgive past hurts?

How many couples would have great meaningful relationships if they would only learn to forgive each other for their mistakes.

If you want to live a fruitful life and experience all that God would have you experience, then live a life of forgiveness.

Release your anger, bitterness and hurt to the Lord.

Give it all over to the Lord, and he will carry your burdens.

Just do it!

Jesus says, in Matthew 11:29, "Take my yoke upon you and learn from me, for I am gentle and humble in heart, and you will find rest for your souls."

The Lord urges us to cast aside all of the loads and burdens we carry and take on His load.

His load is light, and in carrying his burden we will find rest for our souls.

Like I mentioned earlier, forgiveness is a decision, not an emotion.

It is a daily choice, whereby you say, "I decide to forgive and release that person from everything he or she has done."

Forgiveness is the recognition that God settles all scores and the matter is out of our hands.

Forgiveness is realizing that if Jesus could forgive us

for all that we did to Him, than surely we can forgive others.

If you have come to the point where you want to be set free from all bitterness and anger;

if you have come to the point of cutting all ties with the chains that have kept you bound to those who have caused you pain and anguish;

if today is the day you want to experience freedom from a stifled life of being stuck in your cyclone of anger; then take a piece of paper and begin to write down the names of everyone you need to forgive.

Try not to overanalyze it.

If anger exists or any resentment, no matter how small, write it down.

At times, denial sets in and we begin to discount our feelings.

Be focused.

Write it down, no matter how childlike it may seem.

Draw a line from top to bottom dividing the paper into two halves, the left and the right.

On the left side, write down the person's name.

You might want to write down his or her last initial, in case there are many people.

Some might have the same first name.

On the right hand side of the sheet write down, in one or two sentences, their offenses against you.

Try to be factual but not slanderous.

The point here is not to drudge up old hurts, but rather to release those who have hurt you.

Once you have completed this, say the first person's name out loud.

For the purpose of using an example, I will use the name "John."

Say, "John, (for example) I forgive you for saying lies behind my back and accusing me of stealing. John I release the anger I have harbored against you. I release you from your responsibility in causing me pain and embarrassment."

Then proceed to the next person's name and do so in an audible voice.

Remember, you might not feel like you have forgiven these people.

But forgiveness is not an emotion.

It's a decision.

After your mind has decided to forgive, your emotions will follow, and you will feel less angry and bitter towards those individuals.

If you can hardly utter the words of forgiveness, then stop and pray.

Ask God for help.

Ask the Lord for His burden, because it is lighter.

Ask Him to take away your load and replace it with His.

You will find that after a short time, the burden you carry will lighten and what seemed to be an impossible feat will be manageable.

The Lord doesn't want us to survive life.

He wants us to live it.

That is why He calls it life.

It should be lived.

God's desire is that we live life and live it in great abundance.

Jesus says in John 10:10: "The thief comes only to steal and kill and destroy; I have come that they may have life, and have it to the full."

This is God's desire and plan for us.

The only way we can live life to its fullest is by being free.

The only way we can be truly free is be being chainless.

The only way to be chainless is to cut the ties that keep us bound by bitterness and anger.

The only way to be free from bitterness and anger is to forgive.

The only way to forgive is decide to, and then speak it.

As we begin to live a life free from past generational destructive patterns and their sources, we must ask the Lord to help us begin new habits that bring blessings into our lives.

A free life is a blessed one.

Free from addictions.

Free from abuse.

Free from hatred and bitterness.

It implies that we no longer hold on to past hurts and pains that have kept us emotionally bonded to those who have hurt us.

This leads us to our last and final step which we will study in the next chapter: finding a group of healthy friends with whom we can enjoy activities.

Most importantly, these are people with whom we become a better and healthier person.

This is not forced accountability.

This means we find the people that God has destined us to have harmony with.

As we close this chapter together, let us once more ask God for the guidance and strength to forgive us and release all those individuals that we need to forgive.

This is a prayer that might help you as a starting point.

We all need a place to begin.

Let's begin together:

"Lord I know that I have not lived a perfect life.

I know that I have hurt you.

Perhaps I was aware of it or not.

Either way, I know that I have caused you pain.

I ask you to forgive me for all transgressions against you.

I also ask you to forgive me for hurting those who I have hurt without knowing it.

Forgive me for hurting those in past relationships, those in my family, and people who were once friends but are no longer.

As I ask you to clear all the charges against me, I forgive everyone who has hurt me.

Just as you have forgiven me for everything I have done against you and others, I choose to forgive others for what they have done, whether intentional or not.

Lord, give me the strength to make the choice of forgiveness, and help me to live a life free of bitterness and anger.

I ask you to give me your load that is light so that I can live life and live it to the fullest.

I ask these things in your precious name, Amen."

Chapter 6

No man is an island

Several years ago, my wife and I left our three daughters with their grandparents in Southern California.

Cindee and I were heading to a conference in Buenos Aires, Argentina.

After traveling 16 hours through all the necessary connections, we finally landed on the other side of the globe.

We spent a week in crusades and conferences.

Tuesday morning, we were in a church enjoying a great service.

I will never forget the flustered North American who came up behind my wife and me and said, "Um, I don't know if you have heard, but the United States is under attack.

The World Trade Center is demolished, a plane has hit the Pentagon and it looks like another is heading toward the White House."

My heart sank.

I was in disbelief.

I walked out into the church lobby and was told by a good friend, Claudio Friedzon, "Jason, the twin towers are leveled. I saw it with my own two eyes. I saw the second plane hit and watched both towers collapse. Hollywood couldn't have put together a more graphic scene."

My wife and I immediately looked for a television monitor to see what was happening.

There we saw, along with hundreds of millions of viewers around the world, the graphic replays of an unparalleled terrorist attack.

The world was in shock.

CNN announced that the FAA had ordered all flights in the air to land immediately and remain grounded until further notice.

We began to think about how we were going to get back to Southern California to get our children.

We knew we needed to leave Argentina as soon as possible.

We were booked to fly out on September the 12th.

When we called the airline we were using, they said, "We will not be flying for at least a week."

"A week," I thought, "there is no way we are waiting a week to see our girls."

I realized that we needed help.

I realized that we needed a miracle.

We needed family.

We needed friends.

We needed people we could confide in and trust.

No man is an island.

We need friends and family members who can help us get through life.

We need people to help us get from point A to point B.

So I called my in-laws and explained the situation.

The first thing they did was pray and send out an e-mail to a prayer net (a network of people who pray for others in need).

Within minutes, hundreds of people started praying all

over the globe.

I called American Express and asked them for travel assistance.

They not only found a flight into Mexico City, they also patched us through to my in-laws via telephone without charging us.

Considering the long distance cost was $14 for the first minute from Buenos Aires to Los Angeles, we were extremely grateful.

We made reservations to fly to Mexico City on September 13th, two days after the infamous attacks.

We had no flight into Los Angeles, but we would be two thirds of the way home.

The only way we could get home was by a miracle and by friends and family coming to our aid.

We boarded the flight at 1:30 AM, Friday morning and flew directly to Cancun, where we re-boarded and headed for Mexico City.

After landing in Mexico City at noon on September 14th, we would have to drive for twenty-four hours to make it to the San Diego border.

There had to be a better way, but the airways over the United States were closed.

People continued to pray.

Then we had an idea.

We decided to check into direct flights to Tijuana, Mexico.

It's a city that lies just inside the Mexican border and bumps up against San Diego.

We thought, "If we can fly into Tijuana, we can walk across the border, or someone can pick us up."

By another miracle, there was such a flight available several hours after we landed in Mexico City.

There were only two seats available.

We booked the flight and just before we boarded, I

called my father-in-law and asked him to drive into Mexico and pick us up at the airport in Tijuana.

He said, "You can count on me."

The flight was fairly turbulent.

My wife and I could not sit together because it was overbooked.

After landing and exiting the airport, there my father-in-law stood, waving his hand enthusiastically.

We drove three miles until reaching a long line of cars at the border crossing.

It took us two hours to move through the border that under normal circumstances would take five minutes.

We were questioned by two FBI agents who were heavily armed.

The officer said, "Where are you coming from?"

I said to him with a perfect Southern Californian accent, "I'm from Southern Cal, and we were just in Argentina."

We were asked to exit the vehicle and show every piece of luggage and article we were carrying.

After asking us what we were doing in Argentina, they searched the vehicle.

Finally, we were given clearance.

As I crossed the border, I got down on my knees and kissed the ground.

I will never forget that day for the rest of my life.

Because of the hundreds of faithful people who prayed, various companies, my father-in-law and most of all, the Lord, we were able to make it back to our girls during a time of international crisis.

Working as a team is very important; surrounding yourself with friends you can trust is imperative.

Being open and honest with them is even more

important.

Why?

When you have difficulty negotiating your way through life, close friends and family are the backup navigational system that keeps you on course.

Many times, we think that we do not need anyone.

Our life is manageable without any help.

That thought begins at a very young age.

As children, for example, we want to tie our own shoes.

We want to feed ourselves and when we cross the street, we want to do so without holding anyone's hand.

Eventually, we learn to eat alone, cross the street and tie our shoes.

For some things in life, we need very little assistance.

However, as we grow and become adults, we still need support and accountability for overall guidance in our life.

I can't stand forced friendships

For the introverts in this world, there is nothing worse than having to go to a party and meet new people.

You walk in the door and smile at everyone pretending that you are enjoying yourself, when in fact, you would rather be home alone reading a book.

Making new friends can be a painful experience.

For the most part, we are investing time and energy into people without knowing if the investment is worth the effort.

As we talk about forming a support group, so that accountability can reinforce the work that God has done in our life, I am sure the blood pressure will begins to rise in some readers.

The idea of forming an accountability group makes

people cringe.

The thought of having to tell people intimate details of our lives is not their idea of a good time.

Who wants to tell others personal information, especially when we have very little confidence in them?

It is for that reason that I prefer to call such a group a network of trusted friends in whom we can confide.

Instead of trying to force a relationship to be something that it is not designed to be, we should look for friends with whom we feel free from anxiety.

Thus, let me clarify what I mean when I use the term accountability.

It is opening our lives to people with whom we feel comfortable and safe.

Accountability gives such people permission to examine certain aspects of our lives.

We form alliances with them, so they can look out for our spiritual, emotional, psychological and physical health.

These are people who are completely committed to our wellbeing.

Let's say that the CEO of IBM calls and says that the company, a billion dollar multinational organization, has had a complete turnover of leadership.

The shareholders have asked for everyone's resignation.

Thus, the CEO has offered you his job, and the shareholders have ratified you as the new boss.

You've become the Chief Executive Officer.

The entire board of directors has just resigned, as well as all the top executives.

The catch is that if you want the job, you are all alone.

Everyone else has left.

So, you accept the job.

What do you do now?

First, you need to form a team.

It will be impossible to run IBM without great executives and managers.

However, before you hire the people who will help you run the organization, you must put together a list of the necessary qualifications for those who will help manage the company.

Your board must be made up of people of trust, integrity and experience.

If IBM will continue to survive in a highly competitive computer world, there must be a highly unified and qualified team of leadership all dedicated to one solid goal: " ... to lead in the creation, development and manufacture of the industry's most advanced information technologies, including computer systems, software, networking systems, storage devices and microelectronics" (taken from IBM.com).

Imagine trying to fulfill such a mission by yourself.

Impossible.

If you try to manage a company the size of IBM by yourself, the company will go belly up in less than a week.

The same is true for our personal lives.

We need people of integrity, trust and experience surrounding us.

And they must be dedicated to one solid goal: helping us be the best people we can be.

These are the qualifications for the people who should be surrounding us.

They help us grow.

They guide us in the decisions that matter.

They give us the kind of accountability we need.

They keep us on track when the winds of distraction blow us off course.

They help keep us on course when Satan attempts to

lure us into destructive behavior.

A group of caring friends in whom we can confide will help keep our life on a steady course.

They serve as our compass.

Keep your eye on the compass

On August 31st, 1983, Korean Airlines Flight 007 left JFK airport and headed for a refueling stop in Anchorage Alaska.

It departed for its final destination, Seoul Korea, after an hour-and-a-half layover.

Shortly after takeoff, the aircraft deviated off course by perhaps one degree to the North.

This eventually led to the 747 drifting into Russian airspace.

Soviet fighter planes were scrambled to intercept the jumbo jet.

Apparently the Russian defense mistook flight 007 for a spy plane.

Cruising at an altitude of 35,000 feet, the crew of twenty-three had no idea what was in store for them.

Approaching the Kamchatka peninsula, the MIG fighters intercepted the Korean Airliner.

Finally, KAL 007 left Russian airspace and headed toward the Okhostk Sea.

About four hours after take off, the airplane had wandered 185 miles off course and was heading toward Sakhalin.

It re-entered Soviet airspace at about 6:16 PM.

Once again, Russian fighters were scrambled and intercepted the Korean Airliner at about 6:20 PM.

At 6:22 PM the Soviet command center ordered the destruction of the target.

A missile struck the aircraft at 6:26 PM.

Cabin pressure was lost, and the plane started to spiral downward.

Within minutes it crashed into the sea.

All 269 people on board, including passengers and crewmembers, were lost in the Okhotsk Sea.

As I think about this tragedy, I cannot help but contemplate the consequences of making a navigational error by one degree.

A one-degree error at the beginning of a flight is minuscule.

After four hours of flight time (more than 2,000 miles flown) the difference was not minuscule — it was enormous.

After four hours of flight time, the aircraft had wondered off course by nearly 185 miles.

That is almost the width of the state of California.

If the plane had continued for 8 hours, it would have been 400 miles off course.

That is one quarter the width of the United States.

The consequences for wandering off course cost them their lives.

Not keeping their eye on the compass cost them everything.

Their failure to confirm their location with the control tower was their death sentence.

The repercussions for flying blind resulted in the death of 269 people.

Perhaps one degree may not be much at the beginning of a journey.

After time, the difference is staggering.

Most of the 269 people on board would be alive today, if the flight crew had not made the navigational mistake by one degree.

The graph below illustrates how a deviation of one degree becomes great over time.

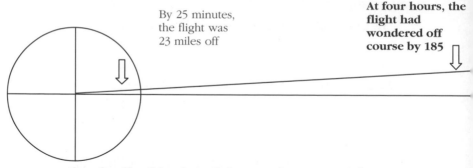

By 25 minutes, the flight was 23 miles off

At four hours, the flight had wondered off course by 185

Our family, friends and the people we trust play a very valuable role in our lives.

They serve as a compass to correct us when we begin to drift off course.

This group of people in whom we confide should desire the very best for our lives.

They are our eyes when we have trouble seeing; our ears when we have trouble hearing; our common sense when we have trouble with our emotions; our sense of direction when we have lost our way; our conscience when our morality becomes questionable; and our wakeup call when we are clueless about being lost.

The helpmate

Marriage is God's primary institution to help keep us on track.

It was designed by God so that two individuals become one flesh.

So then when two individuals commit themselves to marriage, they are supposed to watch over, take care of and help each other through thick and thin.

Regardless of the circumstances, the spouse desires that her husband walk in the right direction.

She is quick to notice when her husband's moral

compass becomes skewed.

She rapidly discerns when he falls into patterns of self-destruction.

The husband realizes when his wife begins to fall into depression.

He is supposed to be her biggest fan and greatest supporter.

No one is quicker to correct, help, straighten out and lend a helping hand when a spouse needs assistance than the mate they're married to.

Together, they form a partnership in which both parties are encouraged to grow and become healthier people.

You can confide in your spouse about your struggles, temptations, resentments, victories, defeats and the intimate details of your life.

There should be no fear to hold things back.

Aside from God, who can you trust more than your spouse?

That is why God designed marriage to progress until death separates the two individuals.

The United States recognizes the institution of marriage and its importance.

A husband and wife, according to the law, have the privilege to preserve the information that spouses share with each other as private and confidential.

A spouse cannot be legally forced to testify against his or her mate.

That is why no district attorney on U.S. soil can call the spouse of an individual to testify in a criminal or civil case without consent.

You can share things with your spouse that you cannot share with anyone else.

You do not have to be concerned that anyone else will hear.

Your spouse is a safe haven.

That is God's design.

Unless there are circumstances where abuse or neglect is occurring, your spouse is a perfect person to include in your group.

As you form a group of supporting friends to help keep your life on course, make your spouse the first member of the group.

Helpful parents

I know that we have talked about the destructive patterns we pick up from past generations.

I have mentioned that parents should not be blamed.

Like I said earlier, this book is not a parental blaming session.

Most parents are wonderful gifts from God, who want the best for their children.

Parents are to be honored.

And we honor them by embracing the good they have handed down to us.

Depending upon the relationship you have with your parents, they can be strategic members of a group of people in whom you can confide.

After all, who knows you better than your parents?

Aside from God and your spouse, who could want the best for you more than your parents?

At the turn of the century, marriages were pre-arranged in many countries.

Why?

Because it was presumed that parents knew their children and knew who would be a better spouse for their children.

I am not sure that we want to go back to those days.

Personally, I think I picked the best possible spouse for

myself, and my parents would agree.

Fifteen solid years of marriage and beautiful children are a testimony to God's blessings upon us.

However, there is one truth that stands out in all of this.

Parents know their offspring and in most settings can give them excellent advice without making them feel threatened.

Do not discount your parents as viable assets to help you in the course of life.

As you reach out to them for council, it will honor them.

Your desire to have their input will tear down walls that have formed over the years.

It will usher in a time of letting the past go, so that you can focus on the future.

As you seek their advice, your parents will feel flattered with the privilege of serving as your advisor.

In short, asking them for guidance honors your father and mother.

Nothing pleases a parent more than when their child comes to them asking for input.

Of course, everyone knows that parents are not perfect.

We are not expecting them to be perfect.

We expect them to give us their best, and in most cases, they will do just that.

This pleases God, because it is part of His design for your life.

God's design is to bring harmony and healthiness to your marriage and to the relationship you have with your parents.

Satan, on the other hand, desires to bring disunity and disorder.

Pitfalls of the enemy

As I mentioned earlier, we live in a war over the very thoughts of our mind.

The war is waged twenty-four hours a day, seven days a week.

The Bible is clear on Satan's position and his desire to destroy life.

It says that he roams the earth seeking that which he may devour.

He demolishes, consumes, and kills.

He works toward that end just as fervently as God works toward healing, restoring, and saving.

Satan uses fear, alienation, and doubt intertwined within anxiety to try to send us to a deeper level of depression.

He constantly tries to infiltrate our minds with lies, in an attempt to bring about greater vulnerability and depression.

One of his greatest tools is to encourage the feeling that we are isolated, so that we feel abnormal.

We have a sense that tells us that no one understands; that we are in this world alone; and that no one really cares.

He bombards our minds with a perpetual negative self-talk suggesting that there is no hope, and that reaching out for help will do no good.

He suggests very subtly that our lives will not improve and that our mental state is in a downward spiral.

There is no hope for change, and no one can help us.

Why do I mention this to you?

Because these are the tactics the enemy uses to keep you isolated, to keep you far from the friends that could potentially help you.

Satan will do anything he can to keep you from a network of friends who will give you guidance and strength.

He will try to convince you that friends cannot help and do not understand.

The devil knows that if you confide in people who will give you objectivity, the perceptions he has thrown your way will be shattered.

He knows that your circle of friends of like faith serve as your radar screen.

They give you pinpoint accuracy on your position.

They tell you if you are heading north, south, east or west.

They tell you if you are off by one or two degrees.

When you wander off course, they can send in air support to escort you to safer skies.

There are two very dangerous tools the enemy uses to keep us away from building Christ-centered healthy relationships, the kind of relationships that keep us on course.

First, he utilizes lies and encourages negative self-talk that ushers our mental state into a downward spiral towards deeper depression.

We hear ourselves saying that we're going crazy or perhaps losing our mind.

We are convinced that things will never get better and thus, we begin to lose our will.

In some cases, people begin to lose their will to live, thinking that change is impossible and that hope is nowhere to be found.

As they become focused inward, they build walls, keeping out friends that could help.

They become convinced that reaching out to others is useless, because no one can help.

The second tool is more devious.

Satan might try to convince you that there is nothing wrong, that you are just simply having "an off day."

You continue in a pattern of self-destruction, not recognizing that a serious problem exists.

You live in denial, grasping on to an optical illusion to divert the pain.

Many people might experience occasional breaks in their emotional pressure.

It is then that people begin to think, "I'm fine." Periodic highs balance out the tough painful valleys.

There are countless examples of people spiraling out of control while reaching out for something that turns out to be a mirage.

Their lives and marriages are falling apart and suffering greatly while they continue with a smile on their face believing that the breakthrough is just over the horizon.

They tell the people with whom they work that everything is fine, while trying to convince themselves that what they are saying is true as well.

I need not mention the names of politicians, actors and even ministers who have suffered such iniquity, trying to pretend that life is "O.K."

Had they reached out to their friends for guidance before their crises, their stories would never have wound up on the front pages of national newspapers.

If we fall prey to Satan's tactics, we stop reaching out to others.

We begin to embrace a survivalist mentality, instead of embracing a mentality of living.

We think, "If I could simply achieve some goal or keep going until the pain passes, then serenity, peace, and contentment will come."

This is nothing more than a ploy to divert attention from the pain, loneliness and iniquity, onto something else, and will only prolong the inevitable: destruction.

And as we put off dealing with these issues, our friends and family suffer tremendously from the emotional distance and superficiality that we embrace.

General pitfalls

In addition to attacks from Satan himself, there are other pitfalls that derail us from living a harmonious life with others.

These are not attacks that come from the enemy, but rather defense mechanisms that surge up from within us.

From time to time a self-defense rises up and tells us that we are not as bad off as we think.

This occurs after several weeks of making decent progress.

You begin to experience a break in the emotional pressure, and thus feel that resolution and restitution has come.

I call it a pre-mature healing.

It is but a taste of what is to come.

But healing and serenity come in stages.

It is somewhat dangerous to view yourself as completely healed after a few weeks.

Experiencing the Power to Change is a process, a partnership between you and God.

Being perfected in Christ is a lifelong process.

It's similar to the pressure that builds up in a two-liter bottle of Coke.

If it has been recently shaken, the first time you open it causes an explosion.

Fizz spews out the top and creates a total mess.

Temporarily, the air-pressure within the bottle has been released.

The bottle is no longer under an extreme burden.

With the lid is off, there is no more spewing.

But after the bottle has been re-sealed, the carbonation in the Coke continues to release gas, and the pressure begins to build once again.

After the bottle is opened again, you can hear the sound of the gas being released.

Depending on how careful you are, the fizz might even spill out again.

This will continue to happen until the Coke becomes completely flat.

In a similar way, after one or two times of getting something off our chest, we feel better.

We lose the need to continue on the road to recovery.

As a result of having a breakthrough, which produces an emotional release and a false sense of total recovery, a person, shortly thereafter, might become ambivalent and lose their sense of urgency about dealing with many of the feelings or events in the past.

They feel like the pressure is gone.

They re-cap themselves, and the pressure begins to build again.

Only until the stuff we are dealing with on the inside becomes flat, can we walk with the assurance that there is no longer a danger of explosion.

A few years back, a young man came to a crusade.

Months before, he had given his life to Christ.

His past was filled with drugs and alcoholism.

God began a great work in his life and immediate family.

After a couple years, several members of his family gave their hearts to Christ.

He became a youth leader in his church.

God had blessed this young man's life.

However, because of all the turmoil of his past, he still carried baggage.

There was a hidden sin that was tearing his personal life apart.

One day, I received a phone call.

My wife and I met with him.

He confessed his sins to us, but I knew one thing was necessary.

He would need a close network of friends to make him accountable.

After the first meeting with me, he said, "I feel much better. I feel great."

Weeks passed, and I did not hear from him.

I discovered that he was struggling again, and I confronted him.

He assured me that he was doing fine.

Later, his pastor told me that he had not been to church in over six weeks.

I confronted him again, but he was convinced that he was fine.

Just like the Coke bottle, some of the pressure in his life was released.

He had a breakthrough.

He felt better.

He felt no need to continue talking about his issues.

He became unaware of his ambivalence.

He lost his need to finish dealing with the baggage he had been carrying for years.

In early 2002, he came by my house and mentioned to me that he had fallen back into the old patterns of self-destruction.

He had entrenched himself, once again, into a life filled with drugs and delinquency.

It becomes easy for us to discount the gravity of our

situation.

Like I mentioned in chapter two, we may have learned to protect ourselves from those who hurt us by forming an emotional wall to numb the pain we experienced.

Many times we may have said, "I will never treat my husband and children like this!"

Raising up an emotional wall severs our connection to the pain.

Our experiences become a mere distant image that is projected as if someone else is experiencing them.

It is as though we are telling a story about someone else's life.

We have completely disconnected ourselves emotionally from the experience.

We respond to our friends in a nonchalant or a matter-of-fact tone.

We speak with total objectivity without any emotional connection.

This is where most of the resistance manifests itself.

As we form alliances with people who can give us guidance, truthfulness is imperative.

We must be completely honest not only about the fact that we need help, but also regarding the facts, events, and emotional pain we have experienced.

We must be transparent.

If we are not honest with our network of confidants, then complete healing will not come.

If we cannot find the problem nor are willing to search for it, then it is impossible to work through it.

We must be completely honest with ourselves, with God, and with those we trust.

Birds of a feather flock together

If you are serious about experiencing new life and attaining God's power to change, you must be ready to make concessions.

You must be ready to make the necessary sacrifices and cut away those elements that are derailing you.

Let's say that your house was built in the 1970s, and the contractors used asbestos.

If you knew that the asbestos was causing cancer to overcome your body, what would you do?

If you wanted to live, you would move out and contract a professional asbestos removal company to safely take out all the hazardous materials.

When it was safe, you might move back in.

Many times, the people we associate with on a regular basis do not encourage us to achieve the best for our lives.

In fact, they are like asbestos.

Our mere association with them causes cancer to begin to develop within us, figuratively speaking.

They encourage damaging behavior that drives the self-destruction further out of control.

At some time in our lives we may have heard the following phrases: "Hey, what you need is a drink ... or several."

Or perhaps, "Let me turn you on to some drugs."

"Go ahead and cheat on your wife. She'll never know."
"Your husband is gone so much. What does he expect you to do ... sit around at home and wait for him? A little fling wont hurt anyone, and it will bring some spice into your life."

Anyone who encourages you to seek a substance over sobriety or an affair over fidelity should be downgraded from a friend to an acquaintance.

If birds of a feather flock together, then we should seek friends that pull us upward not downward.

We should seek healthy friends, not ones that promote destruction in our lives.

A flock of birds can only fly at the pace of the slowest bird.

The friends you surround yourself with will either encourage you to life a godly life or distract you from living one.

You will only be able to fly at the pace of the slowest bird in your flock.

That is why the Bible says in 2 Corinthians 6:14-18:

Do not be yoked together with unbelievers.

For what do righteousness and wickedness have in common?

Or what fellowship can light have with darkness?

What harmony is there between Christ and Belial?

What does a believer have in common with an unbeliever?

What agreement is there between the temple of God and idols?

For we are the temple of the living God.

As God has said: "I will live with them and walk among them, and I will be their God, and they will be my people."

"Therefore come out from them and be separate, says the Lord. Touch no unclean thing, and I will receive you."

"I will be a Father to you, and you will be my sons and daughters, says the Lord Almighty."

There will be those who resist the changes you are embracing.

If they encourage your newfound life, embrace them.

If they try to persuade you to fall back into old routines of self-destruction, it would be best to sever such relationships.

They do not deserve your friendship, because they seek to drag you back into destruction.

Like I said in chapter three, for example, if you have struggled with drug addiction, begin to be selective about the friends you spend time with.

In most if not all cases, it would be best to cut off all drug related relationships.

The same can be said of relationships that center on abusive substance or behavior.

The bottom line

Do you remember the illustration I used in chapter one about the person who had the best seat in the stadium to watch the game?

The person was situated about twenty rows back and had a great perspective in relationship to height and depth to the field.

They sat in the shade so the sun could not affect their vision.

Their seat was perfectly centered between both end zones.

Then, as the game started, they slipped on a welder's shield that prevented them from seeing anything.

All they could hear was the roar of the crowd as one team approached the other's goal line.

Such a person could never enjoy the game.

He or she couldn't see anything.

Their perception of the game would be dark, confusing and at times noisy!

A trusted friend would have leaned over after 30 seconds and said, "What in the world are you doing? Are you nuts? Takeoff that welder's shield so you can enjoy the game. We've paid too much money for you to blow this whole experience."

A good friend would say, "Hey, remove the welder's shield from your face! You are missing the game!"

Ever since 1996, I have been running five times a week.

My cholesterol and blood pressure was a bit high, so the doctor gave me two options.

I could take medication.

Or I could drop some weight, exercise and start eating right.

I opted for the latter.

As a result of eating healthy and exercising, I dropped close to sixty pounds.

My friends said that they hardly recognized me.

It's true.

My body changed a great deal.

For the first couple of years, my friends never asked me how I accomplished my goal.

After three years, however, everyone wanted my regimen.

I had many people wanting to run with me each morning.

People asked me to write down my diet.

Even my doctor wanted to know how I did it.

My cholesterol dropped from 297 to 180.

My blood pressure normalized.

Of the thirty people who have approached me asking if they could exercise with me, several have tried successfully once or twice, but only one has survived for more than a year and a half, my pastor.

Raul Vargas is an interesting character, to say the least.

He is one of my best friends in ministry and a great man of faith.

He has been a great inspiration to me.

But when he first came to me and said, "I want to run with you."

I replied, "That's fine. But I set the pace. I determine the route we take. You can talk to me all you want, but we do not stop to talk to acquaintances along the way."

When I run, I do not stop to talk to anyone, unless it is an emergency.

It's not a social event.

It's not a time for joking around.

Running for me, is an insurance policy that buys me more time with my kids, grandkids (when we get some) and great grandkids.

I made that clear to Raul when we started to run together.

At times, he suggested other easier routes or schedules and I said, "That's OK. I'll run alone."

In other words, I have insisted that we fly upward and not downward.

The goal of our exercise time is to push each other toward greater fitness.

Our relationship has solidified as a result of running together.

Nonetheless, I cannot hold him back, nor can he hold me back.

We need to encourage each other to eat better and exercise our bodies more efficiently.

At the same time, he encourages me as my pastor to run the good race with Christ.

Just like I challenged him to run faster, he challenges me spiritually.

As you pick the relationships that surround you and guide you through life; as you pick a group of trusted individuals who will be real with you; as you pick friends and family to hold you accountable; here is the

bottom line.

Pick relationships that bring out the best in you and lead you toward a better relationship with God, family and friends.

Pick relationships that force you to run more efficiently, fly upward and direct you toward God.

This is God's approach for your life.

Use His approach.

It will bless your life beyond belief.

The heavenly approach

God's approach to these matters is distinct.

His objective for us when we are caught in the patterns of destruction is to restore us to a communion with Him, restore us to a healthy mental and emotional life, and restore us to a healthy relational life with friends and family.

In James 5:16 it says, "Confess your sins to each other and pray for each other so that you may be healed."

God understands the importance of confiding in others, praying for others and confessing your sins to others.

The fifth step in the Power to Change is to form a network of friends, so that accountability can reinforce the work that God has done in your life.

This means that we confess our sins to each other and pray for one another.

We open our heart and support others as they do the same for us.

Our interdependency with others is entirely biblical.

Notice how the Apostle Paul makes an analogy equating the term accountability to a human body.

He suggests that we cannot live life without each other.

He says in 1 Corinthians 12:12-27, starting in verse 12:

The body is a unit, though it is made up of many parts; and though all its parts are many, they form one body.

So it is with Christ.

For we were all baptized by one Spirit into one body — whether Jews or Greeks, slave or free — and we were all given the one Spirit to drink.

Now the body is not made up of one part but of many.

If the foot should say, "Because I am not a hand, I do not belong to the body," it would not for that reason cease to be part of the body.

And if the ear should say, "Because I am not an eye, I do not belong to the body," it would not for that reason cease to be part of the body.

If the whole body were an eye, where would the sense of hearing be?

If the whole body were an ear, where would the sense of smell be?

But in fact God has arranged the parts in the body, every one of them, just as he wanted them to be.

If they were all one part, where would the body be?

As it is, there are many parts, but one body.

The eye cannot say to the hand, "I don't need you!"

And the head cannot say to the feet, "I don't need you!"

On the contrary, those parts of the body that seem to be weaker are indispensable, and the parts that we think are less honorable we treat with special honor.

And the parts that are un-presentable are treated with special modesty, while our presentable parts need no special treatment.

But God has combined the members of the body and has given greater honor to the parts that lacked it, so that there should be no division in the body, but that its parts should have equal concern for each other.

If one part suffers, every part suffers with it; if one part is honored, every part rejoices with it.

Now you are the body of Christ, and each one of you is

a part of it.

Confession is good for the soul

The Apostle John says in 1 John 1:9, "If we confess our sins he is faithful and just and will forgive us our sins and purify us from all unrighteousness."

Because of the mistakes that I had made, I needed to confess my sins and make myself vulnerable to my friends in Christ.

This vulnerability, as frightening as it sounds, is one of the most powerful tools God uses to bring healing and peace into our lives.

We begin to experience normality and acceptance for who we are.

A load is lifted off our shoulders.

The past has been exposed, yet forgiven.

We recognize that we are not the only ones who have suffered.

We are not the only ones who have dealt with tough issues.

The realization comes that everyone has pain in life, and that it is normal to have problems.

For me, it was very refreshing to share my story and have people look me in the eye and say that they were impacted by it.

They had felt alone but later realized that it was normal to struggle.

Everyone has issues.

Everyone has a past.

When I began to open myself in this capacity, I found that no one laughed, chuckled, or talked slanderously behind my back.

I felt accepted, encouraged, and most importantly, normal.

Conversely, as I heard the stories and experiences of others, I too was enlightened by the simple fact that I was human.

The process of sharing our weaknesses and struggles with one another laid a firm foundation for God's healing in my life.

For about six months, I was a part of a small group composed of Christians who came from a similar dysfunction in the home.

They too had struggled.

But instead of worrying about what others would think, we all expressed uninhibitedly the issues we were experiencing.

We operated under an agreement of confidentiality, which prohibited any of us from taking the information shared and broadcasting it outside the walls of our meeting place.

This brought security and trust into our meetings and an atmosphere of openness.

Being able to share in this capacity and meeting on a regular basis helped solidify the accountability and trust.

Most importantly, it solidified God's healing process in us.

Regardless of whether we choose to meet formally with a small group or whether we simply meet with a group of friends on an informal basis, we need to make ourselves fully accountable to others on a regular basis.

Without this type of accountability we can slip very easily back into the patterns of self-destruction we struggled with before.

As you open your heart to a group of people, I would like to offer a very important piece of advice.

If you are not in a group that abides by a confidentiality agreement, you need to feel a sense of trust toward the people you are sharing with.

In other words, you need to feel secure that what you are disclosing is safe and will not be repeated.

Although we need to confide in one another, it will be necessary to exercise caution when you share intimate information.

You need not share gory details to express the truth in words of honesty.

For example, you need not say, "I used to sell drugs to John Doe the politician."

It would be better to say, "I used to sell narcotics to people of every walk of life in our community."

Anyone is capable of deciphering the end result from this information, yet you have not shared the gory details of your mistakes.

Nor have you implicated others.

In a group setting, people need to be honest regarding the fact that they are human.

The intimate details of the mistakes ought to be shared with God and perhaps a counselor.

It is not necessary or advisable to expound on the mistakes you have made by offering copious details.

These are the guidelines that I use as I share my life with others.

Before God, I share everything and every detail of my existence.

That is, nothing is hidden.

If I cannot be honest with God, then I am lying to Him and to myself.

Before a counselor, I am fully clear and accurate about my experiences of pain and answer questions as accurately, cognitively and emotionally as possible.

Otherwise, it is simply a waste of time and money.

With my wife, I feel the liberty to share anything.

In front of a group, however, I need to express the fact that I am human, that I struggle.

I use words that are descriptive yet do not submerge myself into the gory details of the events.

Ultimately, in any setting, I exercise wisdom and ask God for guidance.

Disclosure can be risky at times, but when used with wisdom, it can destroy one of the most powerful attributes of the kingdom of Satan: secrecy.

Because of the mistakes I had made in my life, I thought that the people who knew me would talk behind my back.

I felt that people were saying, "Ah you should have known that guy just a couple of years ago!"

Or perhaps, "I can tell you some things that would shock you about Jason Frenn!"

Or better yet, "He's now calling himself a Christian ... again?"

In the midst of my fears, the Lord encouraged me to begin talking about these issues from the pulpit.

I didn't share any of the gory details, but I did share the struggles of my past, the pain, and the fact that I have made mistakes.

I tried to emphasize that I, like most, am human and have struggled as a Christian.

You may ask me, "Why would you share that?"

I respond with two strong justifications.

First, we have learned from many famous people who have tried to keep secrets about the sin of their life.

Some of them continued in their self-destruction, while refusing to deal with the issues.

Others had corrected their behavior yet tried to conceal their prior wrong doings.

Or perhaps they were unwilling to disclose their failures for fear of the consequences.

Many failed and thus were embarrassed by what gossipers or perhaps the media might say.

177

Many lost their jobs, careers and ministries.

Therefore, I believe that it is necessary to be honest about one's struggles.

This helps us avoid future conflicts with those who wish to bring harm to us.

I began sharing things in my life as a testimony of God's love and forgiveness.

I emphasize the fact that part of my testimony is the work God has done in my life as a Christian.

I tell people that I have struggled just as much, if not more, as a Christian.

Just like I needed Christ when I was fifteen, I need Him every day of my life.

This enables me to minister to many people who are suffering from guilt.

It allows the Holy Spirit to move and touch the hearts of many hurting Christians as well as those who have not come to know Him.

The truth is, God desires to touch not only the hurting sinner but also the hurting Christian who has struggled deeply and perhaps has done worse things as a believer than he or she did before.

Second, without my realizing it at the time, disclosing my struggles helped to accomplish something else.

Today, no one can accuse me of hoarding secrets, nor can they accuse me of lying to the public or to people in the church.

No one can say that I pretended to be something that I wasn't.

I have tried to the best of my ability to confess and disclose my life to my friends, to the public and to the church.

Being honest takes many of the armaments out of the enemy's arsenal.

As a result, I can breathe easier.

I have nothing to hide.

I don't carry guilt.

My load is gone.

I have come clean.

If anyone chooses to judge me for the mistakes I've made in my life, he or she will have to stand before God in judgment and give an account for his or her actions.

The gossiper, in this case, will be revealed as exactly what they are, an instrument of Satan.

A person who is open tears down the walls the enemy has constructed and opens the hearts of those around them.

Over sixty percent of us have lived with or have been closely associated with an addict, and sixty percent of us who have had one or both parents as alcoholics become alcoholics ourselves.

The divorce rate around the world is approximately 50%.

With these statistics it doesn't take much to figure that there is a high percentage of people in our lives that have been touched in some form or another by one or more of these iniquities.

Being transparent about your struggles will help many recognize the sickness in their life and turn to God for healing.

If you can reach out to those in your life in honesty and be vulnerable about who you are, then people will be able to see the iniquity in their own lives.

The naked fireman

On Christmas Eve 2003, we had a wonderful time as a family in Costa Rica.

We lit candles throughout the living room, and the

white twinkling Christmas lights added a nice warm touch to a meaningful time.

We cooked a twelve-pound turkey, cut it into cold cut sizes, and ate around the coffee table next to the Christmas tree.

After reading the story of Jesus' birth in Luke 2, we watched the move, "Home Alone."

Before everyone went to bed, I blew out the candles in the living room and retired to the bedroom.

On Christmas Day, I went for a morning jog.

Afterwards, I jumped into the shower because we were getting together with another family around the noon hour.

I stepped out of the shower and began to dry off.

I wrapped the towel around my waist and headed back to my room.

At that moment, my oldest daughter Celina screamed from the other end of the house, "Mom! Dad! Come here quick!"

I could tell by the tone in her voice that something urgent was happening.

She said, "Come quick!

There is a fire in the living room!"

My worst fear was that the Christmas tree had caught fire and that half the living room was ablaze.

The acoustic ceiling in the living room was made of wood with support beams.

I thought the most terrible thing had occurred.

With the towel wrapped around my waist, I headed toward the distress call.

I jogged down the hall and noticed the smoke pouring rapidly into the hallway.

I turned the corner and entered the living room.

Where a candle had been placed on a wall sconce, a

two-foot blaze was climbing the wall.

Apparently, the night before, we thought that all the candles had been blown out.

Indeed, not all the candles were extinguished.

One candle had a tiny flame that gave off zero light.

The candle burnt the entire evening through Christmas morning.

Finally, the rest of the candle split in two and a pool of wax spilled over the garland.

The flame on the wick caught the garland on fire, and voilàa fire was born.

The candle was gone, and the garland that was wrapped around the base of the sconce was ablaze.

As the flame climbed the wall, it headed toward the garland wrapped over the curtain rods and the curtains themselves.

It was a foot away from igniting it.

I approached the fire and looked around for something I could use to extinguish the blaze.

I saw nothing.

I remembered that I was wearing a wet towel.

So I ripped off my towel, completely exposing myself to the elements, and started beating the flame.

After three or four swipes, the fire was extinguished.

Nothing but smoke rose from the sconce, and there I stood ... completely naked.

I turned around, and my three girls had their faces covered.

I thought to myself, "Well, my girls are going to need therapy after this."

I said, "Girls, keep your eyes covered. Daddy has to put some clothes on."

I had never seen a naked fireman before that day.

I hope to never see or be one again.

Apparently, I blew out all the candles but one.

It was a three-inch thick candle that hung at eye level.

It had a very small flame that burnt down the center of the candle.

The night before, I didn't see any light radiating through the wax.

It was a very small flame.

It was a very small, undetected problem that burned all night long.

A very important lesson stands out from this experience.

Had it not been for my daughter walking by the living room at the perfect time, the entire house might have burnt to the ground.

My daughter's eyes made the difference.

She saw things that I never saw.

She warned me of an impending doom.

She called attention to an area of my life that was in jeopardy, which allowed me to make an adjustment to extinguish the fire.

Without her alerting me, our lives would have changed forever.

In many ways it's like the destructive behavioral patterns in our lives.

Without people around us to help us see the things we cannot see, an impending doom might be right around the corner.

For that reason, we need the eyes of others to help us see things in our life that could destroy us.

How to do it

Let us recognize that times have changed, and the obvious manifestations of the patterns of self-destruction that are passed from one generation to the

next have become more common than ever.

People need more guidance and education in understanding the patterns of self-destruction that Satan has used to bind their particular family.

Regardless of their background, as good as it may be, Christian or non-Christian, people still get caught in the webs of generational patterns of destruction.

For that reason, we need to call for backup.

We need to call in reinforcements.

This is how to do it.

Look around.

Find people who have good moral character, people who are already in your life.

Look for someone who is of like faith and wants the very best for your life.

Do not make intelligence a prerequisite.

You do not want smart people as much as you want people who are wise.

Wisdom is a prerequisite for people you want to surround you.

Chances are, God has already placed some of the right individuals in your work place, school or neighborhood.

There might be a family member or two that can serve in an accountability group for you.

Aside from people in your immediate context, the church can be an excellent source for individuals who can support you.

These are people of like faith.

Spiritually, they will have similar goals.

They want to grow in Christ.

They want to continue to solidify their relationship with God.

They understand the importance of accountability.

Most importantly, they understand what hidden sin can

do to your life.

Take a piece of paper and begin to write down the names of individuals who meet the above criteria.

Think about your family members and friends of like faith.

Think about the people in your life that you admire.

Ask yourself why you admire them.

I would begin to write down every name, starting with people of your own gender.

Depending upon where you are in the process, you might want to meet with just women if you are a woman or men if you are a man.

Sometimes, those of the same sex understand better than anyone else the issues that confront that gender.

Furthermore, accountability groups made up of the same sex eliminate the possibility of people who with deep emotional needs becoming bonded to those of the opposite sex.

All and all, you are putting together a board of directors to help you run the most important company in the world: your life.

I am talking about surrounding yourself with people who will take stock of your life on a regular basis.

I am referring to people who can help you carry the load.

Therefore, pick your team and submit your progress to them.

God will honor you for that.

That is what He means when the He says in Ephesians 5:15-21:

Be very careful, then, how you live — not as unwise but as wise, making the most of every opportunity, because the days are evil.

Therefore do not be foolish, but understand what the

Lord's will is.

Do not get drunk on wine, which leads to debauchery.

Instead, be filled with the Spirit.

Speak to one another with psalms, hymns and spiritual songs.

Sing and make music in your heart to the Lord, always giving thanks to God the Father for everything, in the name of our Lord Jesus Christ.

Submit to one another out of reverence for Christ.

Hebrews 13:16, 17 says:

And do not forget to do good and to share with others, for with such sacrifices God is pleased.

Obey your leaders and submit to their authority.

They keep watch over you as men who must give an account.

If, when you try to assemble a team of trusted friends, you find it difficult to think of anyone, stop and ask God for guidance.

Remember, this is God's will for your life.

No one wants you to live a blessed life more than He does.

He desires that you walk in victory and harmony.

Therefore, ask Him for help.

Ask Him to bring people to your mind that will fill the role.

This is a partnership between you and God.

When you get stuck, He will come through for you.

He didn't rescue you from the river to drown you in the sea.

God will help you finish the job.

As you contact these individuals, tell them that you have turned over a new leaf in life.

Things are going fine, but you would like to touch base

from time to time.

You have a new goal: to live a healthier life physically, emotionally and spiritually.

Tell them that you want to converse with them occasionally about the issues you are facing.

It is not anything formal; you just want to give them the liberty to inquire and help.

You could meet as a group or you could meet one on one.

That depends on you.

As you meet with them, share your new mission in life.

Share where you have come from, where you are going and what you want to avoid in the future.

You can go to a restaurant, coffee shop, mall or park.

At the end of your time, find a place where you can pray about the things you have discussed.

God will bless you as you enhance the relationships in your life and submit yourself to those who can lend an ear and a helping hand.

As we conclude this chapter, I would like to leave you with a final testimony.

My mom has had many struggles and difficulties in her life.

Both of my parents have a great sense of humor.

I think I inherited that from both of them.

Still, my mom traveled through the dark waters of depression during the early 90s.

She survived the death of a spouse, and as a widow, she lived alone for many years.

I can honestly say that of all the five steps suggested in this book, she has not been negligent in any, especially this one: My mother has done an excellent job of establishing relationships in church that have aided her in her spiritual growth.

They have lifted her, not torn her down.

At a time when it could have been very easy to run and hide or shut everyone out, she decided to look in the mirror and seek outside help.

She sought God's help.

She started reading the Bible and praying.

She started to attend a local church.

Lastly, she established healthy relationships with people of like faith.

If my family can overcome the destructive patterns that are passed from one generation to the next; if my family can experience the liberating power of Christ's hand; and if my family can overcome the chains of bondage, then just imagine what God can do in your life.

Imagine what He can do in your family.

Imagine what He can do in your marriage or with your children.

Imagine the possibilities and potential that God has laid out before you.

You are the apple of His eye, and He is rooting for you.

We have been able to partner with God, and He has transformed a family struggling with iniquity.

It was an iniquity ready to be passed from one generation to the next.

It wouldn't have faded out for at least three or four generations.

Instead, the Lord transformed a struggling family into a blessed one that will pass down God's blessings to a thousand generations of those who love Him and keep His commandments.

That is His desire for you and for your family.

This is His word for you as we close this chapter.

Once again, we will end this chapter with a short prayer.

By now, you understand how important prayer is as we reach out to God to be transformed.

Together we will ask God for direction, so that our lives will be surrounded by the right people that can help us with this final step:

"Lord, I thank you that you love me so much.

I realize how fortunate I truly am.

You care deeply about my life, and you want me to stay on track.

It is not your will that I drift off course.

So I ask you to help me find the right friends and people I can trust.

May a group of trusted associates help me keep my eyes on the compass.

Whenever I get blown off course, may they give me the necessary council, so that I do not fall back into patterns of self-destruction.

Help me to find the people that you have destined for my life.

I need your guidance.

I need your wisdom in choosing a network of friends that can be the healthy sounding-board that I need to exercise the power to change.

I ask you to help me see with your eyes and hear with your ears.

I ask you to give me the mind of Christ and the wisdom of God in all things.

I commit my life to you, and I ask this in Christ's precious name, Amen"

Conclusion

He who has ears to hear, let him hear

Recently, a friend of mine sent me an e-mail mentioning a very interesting study done about forty years ago at Yale University.

Two individuals and their family descendants were examined.

Apparently, the study looked at the effects of the lives of these two men upon their children and the generations that followed.

The two men were contemporaries who lived in New York.

One of them did not believe in God and promoted a life of free sex, no laws and no responsibilities.

The second man was known for being disciplined.

He became a preacher and led by strong example.

He authored several books and preached to many people in his lifetime.

Most importantly, he decided to partner with God and the decisions he made were a direct reflection of that partnership.

He married a woman who had deep spiritual convictions and a committed relationship with God.

The results of their values upon their descendants speak for themselves.

The first had 1,026 descendants, of whom 300 were convicts; 190 were prostitutes; 27 were murderers; and 509 became addicted to alcohol or drugs.

To this day, his descendants have cost the State of New York 1.2 million dollars.

On the other hand, the second man had 929 descendants, of whom 430 were ministers; 314 were war veterans; 75 were authors; 86 were college professors; 13 were university presidents; 7 were congressman; 3 were governors; and one was a Vice President of the United States.

One man partnered with God.

The other rejected Him.

One produced descendants that shaped society.

The other created a burden to society.

One chose a life of discipline.

The other chose a life of debauchery.

One walked in the blessings of God.

The other walked in self-destruction.

There is a lesson to be learned regarding how our lives affect the generations that follow us.

If we choose to place substance (alcohol, drugs etc.), debauchery or reckless living over God's laws, we practice idolatry and will necessarily pass that practice and its consequences on to the next generation.

If we fall into patterns of self-destruction, we are not the only ones who suffer.

The generations that follow us will suffer as well.

"He who has ears to hear, let him hear."

Jesus said that more than eight times in the New

Testament.

That was the one phrase He used repeatedly in three of the four gospels.

Why?

He wants to get our attention just before He says something of great importance.

It is a warning sign.

It says, "Hey, pay attention! What I am about to say is of extreme importance!"

Thus I will now say the same: he who has ears to hear, let him hear.

The message that God wants to get across in this book is simple: a life partnered with God is blessed.

A life without Him is plagued with self-destruction, loneliness, depression and alienation.

A life following God's spiritual laws will produce blessings in your family for a thousand generations.

A life filled with idolatry produces emotional and spiritual disaster that will plague the next three and four generations.

The second man in the illustration mentioned above was named Jonathan Edwards.

He was a man who made a difference with his life.

Instead of producing drug addicts, social drop-outs and delinquents, he discipled a family that shaped professors, public servants, ministers, college presidents and authors.

Edwards left behind a great heritage.

It's a heritage that continues to this day.

As you reflect upon your life, what kind of heritage are you leaving behind?

If the historians of the future write a book about you, what will the book say?

If your life were to be studied, would it be considered a blessing for the generations that follow you?

What legacy are you leaving behind?

What are you passing onto the next generation?

I have outlined five stages that will guide you to a life that breaks free from the chains that have bound you and your family.

If you desire to live life and not just survive it, the next five steps will prove to be a fruitful investment.

The truth shall set you free: Step 1

In order for us to leave a great heritage and set into motion a life of blessing, we need to embrace the most important lesson in our journey: truth.

It is the cornerstone of God's Power to Change.

Truth is the foundation upon which we build our godly perceptions.

Without God's truth, our perceptions can be misguided, skewed and contorted.

That is why knowing the truth about ourselves and about the consequences of our actions is imperative.

If we embrace truth, then our perceptions will become clear.

Clear perceptions based upon God's truth are the key to finding freedom, peace and life.

That is why Jesus emphasizes how the truth will set us free as this principle pertains to being His disciples.

John 8:31b, 32 says, "If you hold to my teaching, you are really my disciples. Then you will know the truth, and the truth will set you free."

In essence, being a disciple of Christ is like removing the welder's shields from our faces so we can

see accurately.

His teachings guide us to a clear reality of the way things truly are and what we need to do in order to realize change.

His truth guides us from destructive patterns of self-deception to a life of seeing our lives and the world around us with clarity.

What was once dark and confusing becomes lucid and obvious.

As the clouds part and things become clear, God extends His hand and provides us with a way out of our patterns of destruction.

Sinking to the bottom

When I was about three years old, my mom took me to Malibu Lake in Southern California.

Later in the afternoon, some of her friends joined us for a sun-filled adventure.

The lake was small but surrounded by many luxurious houses.

Many of the Hollywood movie stars lived in the area.

We camped close to a small dock launching out into the lake about seventy feet from the shore.

My mom had warned me not to go out on the mini-pier alone.

Nonetheless, I was determined to go fishing.

While my mom was distracted, I walked out and grabbed a fishing pole.

I had no bait.

I had no lure.

I had no idea how to fish.

So I stuck the pole half way into the water, lost my balance and fell in.

I remember the sensation of falling; it seemed like it was happening in slow motion.

I never closed my eyes.

There was a cloud of green algae swarming around my face reducing my visibility to about three inches in front of my nose.

I squinted upward and noticed the light from the sky slowly diminishing as I sank to the bottom.

I was disoriented and unable to help myself.

I felt like I was stuck in a cesspool of green slime.

A feeling of fear overwhelmed me, because I was unable to see.

The slimy algae that stuck to my eyes prevented me from seeing anything.

For a few seconds everything was dark, dark green to be precise.

One person saw me fall in and called for help.

People began to run down to the end of the dock.

Ever since I was a baby, I had been around the ocean.

I knew how to swim.

Knowing how to swim wasn't the problem.

I had lost my point of reference completely.

I lost my ability to decipher which way was up or down, left or right.

My eyes and equilibrium were thrown into a complete frenzy.

I lost my navigational system.

I was disoriented.

I was lost.

That was my problem.

Slowly but surely, I started to rise to the surface.

That is the wonderful thing about water.

Eventually, you either float or get washed ashore.

Being that I was a chunky little boy, I floated fairly well.

After about ten very long seconds, my little noggin and baby blue eyes popped out of the water.

Finally, I regained my orientation, although I couldn't see that well.

I gasped for air.

I could hear people screaming, "There he is."

I was able to keep my head above the surface without assistance, but I had one final obstacle to overcome.

I was incapable of climbing out of the water.

The dock protruded out of the water about 18 inches above the surface.

My arms were too short to reach.

I was fully dressed and completely waterlogged.

My clothes were like a wet ball and chain.

There I was, stuck again.

So I looked up with desperation in my eyes for someone to help me.

That is when I saw a hand extending out for me.

A friend of my mom reached down, grabbed me and placed my safely on the dock.

That person saved me from drowning.

There I stood with a gush of water flowing out of my clothes onto the dock.

About a half a dozen people were looking at me with a look of bewilderment as if to say, "You must be the most fortunate kid in the world. We thought you were a goner."

Having the right perception:

Step 2

Similar to falling into an algae-filled lake, people can fall into patterns of self-destruction and lose their orientation entirely.

Many are unaware that they are lost.

They keep sinking until they reach the bottom.

The algae-of-life blocks their vision.

Like a little boy sinking to the bottom of a lake, they lose their perception.

What they need is God's perception, realizing that change is not only necessary but also possible.

That is where the battle lies.

For most, we recognize that change is important but find it hard to believe it is possible, especially as we sit at the bottom of a lake blind and waterlogged.

As the sensation of losing oxygen increases, so does our anxiety.

In most cases, people reach out to drugs and alcohol.

Instead, we need to reach out to God and ask Him to give us a change of perception.

Too many models lose their lives to anorexia.

Too many politicians lose their place of public service to marital infidelity.

Too many business executives lose their jobs to alcoholism.

Too many athletes lose their careers to drugs.

Too many young people lose their lives to violence.

Too many celebrities lose their lives to suicide.

Why?

They all sit at the bottom of a lake, without air.

When anxiety or depression sets in, they turn to some sort of idolatry to ease the pain.

Because they are blinded by the algae pressed up against their eyes, they feel lost and completely disoriented.

When we fall into the lake of life and feel like we are drowning, we need God to reach in and pull us out.

That is precisely why Jesus came.

He came to pull us out of the cesspool in which we live, to give us eternal life.

He came to redeem us from the slime and self-destruction that binds us and our families.

Jesus leans over the edge of the dock and extends His hand to you.

He is ready and willing to pull you out.

Take His hand, and he will lift you to Himself — to safety.

Having the right habits: Step 3

Like I mentioned earlier, Jonathan Edwards made a difference with his life.

He passed down the blessings of God to the generations that followed him.

Instead of embracing chaos and debauchery, he held onto the laws of God.

That made the difference in the lives of thousands who followed him.

I am sure that most people would like to leave a legacy like Edwards.

So how do we get beyond the crazy cycles of self-destruction, the ones that are passed from generation to generation?

Realizing the source of our chaos and dealing with it is simply the beginning.

Putting into practice new habits that replace old ones becomes the next step.

In 1996, we held our third open-air crusade in a marginalized community called Los Cuadros, Costa Rica.

The day before the event, we set up the stage, lighting and took care of all the logistical needs.

Afterwards, I headed home.

The pastor arranged for five guards to watch over all the gear until the following day.

At about 11:30 p.m., I received a phone call that woke me up out of a deep sleep.

I do not wake up quickly, so I hardly remember the conversation; however there are several things I do recall.

The person who phoned me was the pastor's wife.

She said, "Jason, do you remember the platform that you left up here in Los Cuadros?"

I said, "Yes."

She said, "Do you remember all the sound and lighting gear and cabling?"

I said, "Yes."

She said, "Do you remember all the electrical cables and the electrical connections hooked into the transformer?"

I said, "Yes."

She said, "Do you remember the five guards we left to watch over all your gear?"

I said, "Yes."

She said, "The guards are gone!"

I said, "What do you mean they're gone?"

She said, "You heard me. They're gone. A gang came and roughed them up pretty badly. They cut off the ear of one of the guards, and he is in the hospital. All of the others ran off."

"In short, there is no one watching over your crusade equipment. So if you want to have anything left by morning, you better get up here and watch over the gear yourself. Right now, my husband is out looking for anyone who would be willing to stay the night and guard the equipment until morning. But until he finds about ten people, we need someone to be at the site."

So I agreed to go up to the lot and watch over the gear until the pastor could substitute me with other guards.

I put on my exercise outfit: Nike shoes, Nike socks, Nike shorts and a Nike t-shirt.

Like I said, I do not wake up fast.

I jumped into my minivan and headed up the mountain to one of the most dangerous communities in all of Central America, dressed like the Nike Poster-boy.

When I arrived at the site, no one was there.

It was vacant.

I walked up the stairs of the platform and began to wander around the stage nonchalantly checking the setup.

At that moment, I thought that it would the best use of my time if I would simply pray for the crusade and for the community.

I asked the Lord to set people free from the bondages of drug addiction, gang violence and delinquency.

Suddenly, a cool breeze kicked up, and I began to wake up.

I realized where I was.

I realized the time.

I became aware of the neighborhood in which I stood.

And I remembered how I was dressed.

Suddenly, I looked off the starboard side of the platform and saw 25 individuals emerge from the darkness in a community infested with violence and drugs.

The leader stepped forward and said, "What do you think you are doing?"

With a bit of terror in my voice I said, "Um, I'm guarding the gear."

Ironically, they laughed.

At that moment, a minivan approached.

It was the pastor with eight new guards and a few guard dogs to boot.

I said, "Whew. Look at the time. I am outta here."

As I was making my way to my vehicle, the leader made eye contact with me and said, "We'll see you tomorrow night."

Something told me that he was not going to show up to worship the Lord.

The first night began.

During the first three songs, we had a half a dozen rocks exploding like hand grenades onto the platform.

The gang had come to wreak havoc and did not come to "Praise the Lord."

We had a youth team from Lancaster California.

For security reasons we decided to ask them if they wouldn't mind staying on the bus.

Once they were inside, we secured it with a padlock.

During the music, some of the gang members walked behind the platform and starting shaking the bus that was parked six inches behind the stage.

They rocked the bus slamming it into the stage.

It was like preaching during an earthquake.

Ten feet from the platform stood a drug dealer.

He was trying to sell crack to an undercover cop, who kindly said, "You're under arrest."

The dealer refused and threw the cop up against the wall.

As he ran off, he didn't see the other undercover officer hiding behind our stage.

The officer jumped out, grabbed him and threw him to the ground.

He then pulled out his nunchucks and beat the drug dealer as brutally as anything caught on videotape.

As if that was not enough for excitement, before I started to preach, a gang member had brought a crow bar onto the crusade lot and walked up to an enemy gang member and struck him on the head.

He nearly split his skull in two.

I thought, "This is the most exciting service I have ever been a part of in my life."

Two donut shaped circles formed and a huge fight broke out.

At that moment I grabbed the microphone and gave a strong rebuke to everyone who didn't respect the fact that we were in "God's house."

The fight dispersed, and I started to preach.

About halfway through the message, the five most feared gang leaders walked onto the lot.

Up until that point every other gang member was a peon in comparison.

When these five individuals walked across the lot, people moved out of their way, including security and pastors.

Eventually, they planted themselves at the base of a light tower and began searching for the kid who had the crow bar.

They had come to settle the score.

Their philosophy was "an eye for an eye and a tooth for a tooth."

At some point during the message, they became very displeased with what I was saying.

I could tell by their demeanor that they were becoming upset.

I feared that I would be having a face off with them after the service.

Needless to say, I wasn't too excited about that.

Across the street a young man was sitting on his roof listening to the message.

I continued to preach and remember making the following statement: "You may hear voices in your head telling you to kill yourself. But I am here to tell you that Jesus has come to silence those voices and give you freedom and peace. He has come to set the captive free. Take His hand, and He will set your free."

The young man would later tell me that he had been planning to take his life later that night.

The words I shared that night were exactly what he needed to hear.

As a result, he came down off the roof, came to the altar call and gave his life to Christ.

I remember vividly the moment I asked those who wanted to make a commitment to the Lord to come forward.

At that instant, an usher stood to his feet and walked back to the light tower.

He, alone, approached the five gang leaders who were watching me with disgust in their eyes.

He stood before them and said, "We all know each other."

"We grew up together in this community. You know my brother as well. He is a drug addict. If he doesn't change his life, he is going to die in the streets, just like some of you. Unfortunately, you have brought nothing but violence and destruction into this neighborhood."

"If you had any sense whatsoever, you would take the advice of the preacher up on the platform and make a commitment to Christ."

They somberly looked ahead but continued to listen.

He continued, "I know that you want to leave this crazy self-destructive lifestyle, and I believe that if we could pray together, God would set you free from all the mental torture you face on a daily basis. I would like to pray for you. May I?"

As the leader looked the usher in the eye, he paused for a moment and glanced downward.

He removed his ball cap, and the others followed suit.

They all bowed their head.

Then, he began to ask the Lord to intervene in their lives.

He asked the Lord to break the chains of all addiction and bondage.

He asked the Lord to give them the strength to walk away from a life of destruction.

He asked the Lord to give them the strength to lead a life of blessing.

Then he stopped and said, "I feel that if we all ask the Lord for forgiveness, He will free us from the spiritual chains that have been binding us. Why don't we ask the Lord to forgive us together?"

At that time, I was praying with those who had come forward to make a commitment to Christ.

When I looked up, I saw something that shocked me, to say the least.

I saw the usher and all five gang leaders on their knees

asking God for forgiveness.

When they had finished praying, they came down to the front and said to me, "Jason, we just wanted to ask you for forgiveness.

You see, we had planned to destroy this whole place, but you don't have to worry about that now."

Needless to say, I breathed a huge sigh of relief.

So much craziness — so much violence — so much destruction.

Especially for one night.

All of it was transformed within minutes by the power of God's love.

Christ broke the chains of destruction and madness and turned hearts that were leading a life of hatred into hearts of love.

Hearts that once embraced anger were transformed into hearts filled with peace.

Hearts that were fueled by resentment were changed into hearts permeated by God's forgiveness.

Hearts that were hurt became healed.

God touched hearts swimming in chaos and turned them into hearts soaring with purpose.

One week after the crusade, I was awakened by another phone call.

Guess who.

It was the five ex-gang members.

They said, "Is this Jason Frenn?"

"Yes," I replied.

The leader said, "Hey, I know its real late, but I just called you to tell you that we are all doing great. We just got out of a prayer meeting. God is so good, isn't He?"

I said, "Yes, He sure is."

He said, "Hang on a second, Juan wants to say 'Hi'."
Juan got on the phone and said, "Oh man, God is great! He

is transforming my life! Hang on, Carlos wants to say 'Hi'."

Carlos got on the phone and said, "My life was a disaster, but Christ has set me free! God is so good! Hang on, Roberto wants to say 'Hi'."

I talked to all five guys for ten minutes and the topic of the conversation was: "God is so good!"

Indeed, God is good.

All five left their gang and within six months became leaders in the local churches of Los Cuadros.

To this day, the gang violence and organized crime in Los Cuadros has never been the same as it was prior to that crusade.

The suicidal teenager who came down off his roof to commit his life to Christ was not exempt from the power of God that night.

He too realized the Power to Change.

He told me that within days of his experience with Christ, all of his suicidal thoughts began to fade away.

New patterns began to emerge as he began to walk with Christ, read the Bible, attend a local church and surround himself with friends of like faith.

For the last eight years he has been a youth leader in his church, working with a ministry for boys called Royal Rangers.

Each and every one of these individuals found the source of their patterns of self-destruction, and God helped them deal with their pain.

But most importantly, they were able to move beyond it and do something significant with their lives.

They moved away from their idolatry and dependence on drugs and made God the center of their world.

Each and every one replaced the habits of self-destruction with the habits that God prescribes in His word.

They personify God's Power To Change.

The Power to Change is simply a matter of taking responsibility for your life and partnering with God.

It means that you take a good hard look at yourself and ask God to help you move away from self-destruction.

It means that you begin to walk in harmony with God's laws.

As a result, you begin to experience His blessings not only for you but also for the generations that follow.

Although seeing things differently and putting new habits into practice is imperative, it is the halfway point in your transformation.

You also need to inventory your hurts and pain and release all bitterness and anger.

The gang members and the suicidal teenager were able to forgive many who had hurt them.

They took the fourth step: letting bygones be bygones.

Letting bygones be bygones: Step 4

Up to this point, we have learned the importance of renewing our perceptions and seeing things from God's view.

The truth is the most important ingredient to seeing our lives as they truly are.

As we partner with God to realize change, He helps us arrive at the source of the conflicts that have been keeping us in chains.

We begin to re-write the scripts and patterns of self-destruction, replacing them with godly ones.

This carries us to the fourth step, which requires that we be forgiven and forgiving others.

Forgiveness is one of the main points of Christ's teachings in the New Testament.

He understood that if people wanted to be free, they would have to forgive those who caused them pain.

2,000 years later, the importance of forgiveness remains the same.

So many people today carry anger for years and continue to stay bonded to those who have hurt them.

Now more than ever, people need to hear the message of forgiveness.

In order for us to be free, we need to forgive all debts.

When these debts are forgiven, we walk in freedom.

We no longer carry the burdens that have weighed us down.

Back in March of 1999, my wife and I were planning to return to the United States from Central America for a year of itineration (traveling across the country to raise our ministerial budget).

I remember sitting in a conference for ministers and writing in my prayer journal that we needed a financial miracle before we could return to California.

At that time, we needed approximately $5,000 in order to purchase a vehicle, set up an apartment and if anything was leftover, buy some clothes for the family.

March passed.

April passed.

Nothing came in.

Our departure date was May 24th.

The last weekend we were in Costa Rica I preached in our home church Oasis de Esperanza (Oasis of Hope).

I remember that night vividly.

One of the ushers in the church came up to me and

asked if she could polish my shoes.

She said to me, "Jason, would it bother you, if I cleaned up your shoes? It's just that they seem to be a bit too dirty."

To be completely honest, I was not humiliated.

My shoes were old and in terrible condition.

I think my wife was more mortified than I was.

But at that time you could not find size twelve in Costa Rica.

So I had to use what I had.

I sat down in the back of the church, and while she polished them, she told me that I should take better care of my shoes.

Afterward, I thanked her, and she returned to her post.

That night, I shared a simple message on how God was the God of second chances.

When I finished, the associate pastor came forward and said that the church was going to receive an offering for us.

He told me to use it however we seemed fit.

The offering was $1,000.

I was grateful to the church for its generosity and grateful, of course, to the Lord.

The week prior to our departure, I knew that we still needed $4,000.

That is when I received a call from my father-in-law, asking if I would be interested in translating for a friend of mine.

It was a crusade in California scheduled the day after we were to arrive.

The coordinators needed someone to interpret from Spanish to English.

I felt honored by the invitation and told him that I would be glad to help.

Five days later, on May 24th, we headed back to Southern California.

That night we ate at the famous Cheesecake Factory in Newport Beach.

It was a beautiful night and a great way to return home after four years of serving overseas.

Early the next morning, I was awakened around 4:00 AM by terrible stomach pains.

Like I do every morning, I ran two miles, but the pain was as persistent as ever.

On my final lap, I asked the Lord to intervene, knowing that I was going to translate that night at a major event.

It was amazing.

After five minutes, the pain began to disappear.

About noon, we headed to the crusade and stopped at a shopping mall along the way to purchase new shoes.

I didn't want anyone at the crusade to see my toes pushing through the soles.

The first night of the crusade went well, but I felt fairly exhausted.

The second night was much smoother, and the preacher did an outstanding job in communicating his message.

The morning following the crusade, both the preacher and I were invited to eat breakfast with the pastors who had sponsored the crusade.

So I took all three of our girls to the restaurant.

After we finished eating, the coordinator said, "Thank you so much for serving us in this capacity. You have truly blessed our hearts."

After giving an envelope to the speaker, he turned and gave one to me as well.

I assumed that it was an offering for serving as the interpreter of the event.

So I asked if I could apply whatever was in the envelope to any particular need we had.

He replied, "Of course."

After saying goodbye and exchanging hugs, I said to the girls, "Come on. Let's go for a walk on the beach and find a park."

The girls were excited.

Along our park-seeking journey, I began to wonder what was in the envelope.

Normally, I do not open a check for an offering in public.

I didn't want to give any of the pastors the wrong impression.

So about 10 minutes later we found a set of swings and a jungle gym.

The girls immediately started climbing like monkeys turned loose in a tree.

I pulled the envelope out of my pocket and thought, "Well there's probably a check for $250 to $300."

So I opened the envelope and unfolded the check.

What did the check say?

At first, my eyes couldn't believe it.

"This can't be right," I thought.

The dollar amount read "$4,000.00."

I rubbed my eyes for a second to ensure that my vision was clear.

Then I focused on the portion where the check writer has to spell out the amount on the check.

It read: "Four thousand dollars and ----------- xx/100."

The next thing I recall, my girls huddling over me, waving their hands in front of my face and saying,

"Daddy, are you OK?"

In other words, I had almost passed out.

I jumped up and screamed, "Hallelujah. God is our provider!"

Indeed He is our provider.

I danced around that little park, just like Peter Pan after defeating Hook.

In one powerful blow, God erased every financial need we had.

There was enough money for us to purchase a vehicle, set up an apartment and buy some clothes for the entire family.

I was so excited.

We were all excited.

About six weeks passed as we embarked upon the itineration trail.

We were driving from California to Tennessee and spent the night in a hotel in New Mexico, when I received a call on my cell phone.

The voice on the other end seemed very serious, sort of like Officer Friday on the old TV series, "Dragnet."

He said, "Is this Jason Frenn?"

I replied, "Yes."

Without hesitation, he said, "I am the accountant for the crusade you helped us with six weeks ago.

I understand that you were the translator.

By chance when you received an envelope with an offering, was it a check for the amount of $400?"

Time stopped.

The world stopped.

Or perhaps it was just me.

There I was, sitting in a hotel room on my cell phone somewhere between Albuquerque, New Mexico and Amarillo, Texas.

The girls were out at the pool with my wife.

I felt like a fugitive.

I felt as though the rug had been yanked out from under me.

I thought, "Houston, we have a problem!"

I took a deep breath and said, "No! No! The check you wrote out to me was for the amount of $4000."

He said, "Well, there has been a huge mistake, a $3,600 mistake to be exact."

I said, "The check you wrote out to us was for the amount of $4,000. When I opened it, I looked and both amount areas had the same quantity."

He replied, "We need to resolve this problem. Are you sure about the amount?"

Then I took a deeper breath and said, "Last March I wrote down in my prayer journal that we needed exactly $5000 so that we could return to the States, purchase a vehicle, setup an apartment and buy some clothes for the family for our year of itineration."

"The last week we were in Costa Rica, our home church gave us a personal offering for $1,000. We received a phone call saying that a translator was needed for the crusade. Literally, the day after we landed in Southern California, I drove to the crusade and translated both nights. The day following the event, the coordinator handed me a check for the exact amount that we needed in order to make this year a possibility. However, if you are saying that the check amount was a mistake and that we need to give you back the difference, I am going to need a little bit of time. Because that four grand ... is gone."

There was a long pause on the other end of the phone.

After about five seconds, he said, "If you are telling me that you needed exactly $4,000, and the Lord led me to write out a check for that exact amount, then that must be God's will. Keep the $4,000. I'll figure out how I will manage things on my end. God Bless you!"

Then he hung up.

In six short weeks we went from needing $4,000 to having all debts erased to owing $3,600.

What a roller coaster!

When all the dust settled, however, it was amazing to be forgiven.

The feeling of having a debt forgiven is incredible.

When someone says to you, "Don't worry about the money you owe. I'll take care of it on my end."

There are no words to describe your appreciation.

One becomes overwhelmed with gratitude.

In the same way, Jesus died on the cross for you and me.

He paid every spiritual debt and sin we have ever committed in our lives.

He says, "There is no way for you to repay the debt. Therefore, don't worry about it. I already took care of it on my end — on a cross."

Just like the accountant for the Claudio Friedzon crusade forgave us a $3,600 oversight (a slipup for them, but a miracle for us), God forgives us and wipes the slate clean.

But just like the Argentine Dance, one person cannot do the tango.

It takes two to tango

Forgiveness is a two way street, and the Bible calls for us to forgive in the same way we have been forgiven by God.

We cannot simply receive forgiveness and guard resentment and anger toward others.

That would perpetuate a cycle of self-destruction in our lives.

Bitterness and anger will grow in the orchard of our heart, and the victims are not those who we hate — we are.

Bitterness and anger are poisons we drink, hoping that our offender will die.

This only hurts us and, ironically, keeps us firmly bonded to those who have offended us until the day we release them.

Further, forgiveness is not dependent upon whether the offender looks for or desires forgiveness.

Just like we freely receive it, we freely extend it.

The Bible is clear on this as it states in Luke 11:4 "Forgive us our sins, for we also forgive <u>everyone</u> who sins against us."

Just as we receive forgiveness, we extend forgiveness to everyone who has offended us.

This is God's plan.

This is His good will.

This is God's deal with us.

Forgiving others will reap incredible benefits for our personal, emotional, physical and spiritual lives.

Forgiving and being forgiven releases a weight off your emotional shoulders that cannot be measured.

It sets the stage for the final step in your transformation: living your life like an open book.

Living your life like an open

book: Step 5

In my personal life, there are very few things that I will not disclose.

I try to live my life like an open book.

I find that in doing so, I am in less danger of getting off course.

As you allow others with whom you are accountable to see your life for what it truly is, they will help keep you on the straight and narrow.

Forming a group of godly individuals to give you guidance and leadership is one of the most important steps in your transformation.

If you conceal your actions and values, you stand in great danger of drifting off course.

Drifting off the course of life, sooner or later, will prove to have deadly consequences for you and those closest to you.

Thus, we need the eyes, ears and senses of people of like faith to give us direction.

We need their objectivity in times of turbulence and transition.

Over the past five years, I have flown over 120,000 miles.

Some airlines allow their passengers to listen to air-traffic conversations between the control tower and cockpit.

A few years back, we were on a flight from Chicago to John Wayne Airport in Santa Ana, California.

Cruising at an altitude of 39,000 feet, approaching the deserts of Southern California, the control tower told our flight crew to begin our decent to a flight level of 20,000 feet.

It was a beautiful day in Southern California.

There wasn't a cloud in the sky.

The visibility was at least sixty miles.

As we approached San Bernardino, the control tower continued to lower our flight level until we reached the city of Orange.

There, we were instructed to lower our altitude to 5,000 feet.

We were on our five-mile final approach and coming up on a helicopter marine base located in Tustin.

The descent into John Wayne is somewhat tricky, due to noise regulations and heavy air traffic in the area.

In addition to avoiding the air traffic from the marine base and noise abatement, our flight was battling crosswinds.

All of a sudden, I heard the control tower say to our pilots, "Flight number 251: turn left ten degrees."

There was no response from our flight crew.

The control tower repeated, "Flight 251: turn left ten degrees for traffic."

Again, there was no response.

Finally, the control tower exclaimed, "Flight 251 turn left immediately!"

As the first officer responded, I could hear a warning signal going off in the cockpit through the radio transmission.

He replied, "We're on it!"

The plane banked hard to the left, and on the opposite side of the aircraft, my youngest daughter said, "Look, Mommy, a plane."

A small Cessna was heading for a collision course with our 757 just three miles from the runway.

We banked to the left just in time.

If the pilots had not heeded the control tower's call, it would have been a very tragic day!

One minute the flight was uneventful.

Seconds later, we almost had a midair collision.

Nothing impeded the pilot's vision.

There were no clouds, no smog and it was almost noon.

Think about it for a moment.

How many "close calls" have you had in a car or while crossing the street?

For me, the times are innumerable.

If your car had crossed the intersection seconds before (when the other vehicle ran a red light), your life would have been severely altered.

Your group of friends will serve you well and keep you on the course of life.

Just like the tower served as the eyes for a plane flying blind, even on a clear day, your group of friends will guide you into a runway whether the weather is great or not.

You need them.

This is God's plan for you.

So then, live your life like an open book.

Your godly friends will help to keep you on God's course for your life.

Without them, a tragedy could be just around the corner.

A final word

Finally, I want to say to you: stay the course.

The wind will blow and turbulence will make the air around you unstable.

But God will give you the guidance you need.

He will be a satellite that gives you an accurate reference.

Expect delays.

Changing your life is not done overnight.

It is done one day at a time.

Many of the patterns of destruction in which we find ourselves take years to form.

Therefore, it might take a bit of time to move beyond them.

In many ways, realizing the Power to Change is similar to going on a diet.

If it takes us 20 years to gain 50 pounds, we cannot lose that weight in a week.

Just remember, God is in your corner, and you will win the good fight.

Therefore, "He who has ears to hear, let him hear."

In the fight of life, no one has fought to get your attention as much as God.

No one has sought to pull you out of the gutter like the Lord.

You were created to be His son or daughter.

That is His plan, because you are the apple of His eye.

He desires to turn your disasters into victories.

He wants to see your children walk in His blessings.

The depression and alienation that you have suffered can be broken through the partnership you form with Him.

No one desires that your life be blessed more than God.

No one wants to help you more than Him.

No one has yearned to help you more than Him.

No one wants you to experience new life more than God.

That is why I wrote this book.

The only true solution for breaking the chains of oppression, addiction and dysfunction is the power that Christ gives us through a daily relationship with Him.

Many other solutions can work, but only temporarily.

Only Christ can truly deliver.

Only He can grant life in abundance, allowing you to LIVE.

That is precisely my desire for you.

That is my prayer for your life.

I ask the Lord to grant you new life.

I don't want you to survive life.

My desire is that you LIVE IT.

In every chapter I have written out a prayer that you can use as an example.

This time, I want to close out this book and our time together praying for you:

> "Lord, I lift up my friend before your throne and ask you to fill every gap in his or her life.
>
> May you touch this life and set it free from every source of bondage.
>
> I pray that you will silence every source of negative self-talk and all the diabolical voices that are swarming around in the thought patterns of my friend's heart.
>
> May the attacks of the enemy cease and immediately begin to recede.
>
> I pray that you would reveal every source of destruction cultivating in their heart so that it can be removed.
>
> Initiate godly practices and keep them unto yourself, protecting them from spiritual disaster.
>
> Give them the strength to live a life of forgiveness and freedom from all bitterness.
>
> Surround them with people who will keep

them accountable and on the right course with you.

I ask that their past, present and future leave a legacy of your strength and testimony.

Finally, I ask that those who love you and keep your commandments would be highly blessed for a thousand generations.

I ask this in your precious and Holy name, Christ Jesus, Amen."

May God richly Bless You in every area of your life!

Taking it to The Nations

Salvation, healing, deliverance and restoration are foundational elements in the Gospel. Jesus set the captive free. He saved, healed and restored people. Why? Because He loves them. Our biggest desire is to share the love of God with a hurting world. We have been asked to continue holding massive public evangelistic meetings throughout Latin America. Please visit our web site to see how you might become a part of this exciting ministry to reach people who need to hear that Jesus has come to set the captive free.

Jason & Cindee Frenn
Founders of *Taking It To The Nations Ministries*

Join With Us...

in the great commission playing an active role in these crusades. If you would like to send financial support, please send your offering to:

Jason & Cindee Frenn Ministries
AGWM 244598
1445 Boonville
Springfield MO 65802

www.frenn.org